SIXTY
YEARS
OF
INTERIOR
DESIGN

A STUDIO BOOK·The Viking Press·New York

SIXTY YEARS OF INTERIOR DESIGN

The World of McMillen
by Erica Brown

Preface by Walter Hoving

Also by Erica Brown *Interior Views: Design at Its Best*

First published in 1982 by
The Viking Press (A Studio Book)
625 Madison Avenue, New York, N.Y. 10022
Published simultaneously in Canada by
Penguin Books Canada Limited

Library of Congress Cataloging in Publication Data
Brown, Erica.
    Sixty years of interior design.
    (A Studio book)
    Includes index.
    1. Brown, Eleanor McMillen. 2. McMillen Inc. 3. Interior
decoration—United States—History—20th century. I. Title
NK2004.3.B76B75   729   82-70185
ISBN 0-670-64775-6   AACR2

Grateful acknowledgment is made to the following for permission to
reproduce copyrighted material:

The Condé Nast Publications Inc.: Photographs on pages 185–87
by Anthony Denney; on pages 210–15, 217, 218, 220, 221, 223, 224
by Tom Leonard; on pages 232, 262 by Tom Yee; on pages 233,
262, 265, 266, 268 by Horst; all courtesy *House & Garden.* Copyright © 1952, 1964, 1970, 1971, 1972, 1974, 1975 by the Condé
Nast Publications Inc. Photographs pages 172–75 by André Kertész,
courtesy *Vogue.* Copyright © 1949 (renewed 1977) by the Condé
Nast Publications Inc.

The New Yorker Magazine, Inc.: A selection from "About the
House," from the April 19, 1952, issue of *The New Yorker.* Copyright © 1952, 1980 by The New Yorker Magazine, Inc.

Black-and-white pages printed in the United States of America
at Murray Printing, Westford, Massachusetts
Color pages printed in Japan
at Dai Nippon Printing Co. Ltd.

Set in Electra

Book designed by Michael Shroyer

FRONTIS: Eleanor Stockstrom as a
debutante in St. Louis in 1908.

Acknowledgments

Like many undertakings, putting together this book proved more complicated than I had first anticipated. The fact that it was, throughout, a pleasure owes much to the help and encouragement I received from all concerned.

Michael Dunne, whose work accounts for almost half the color photographs in this book, kept his extraordinary sense of picture composition, his eye for detail, and his sense of humor throughout almost a year of shooting—even when asked to fly more than twelve hours from London to Palm Beach via New York, arriving at 11:30 P.M. local time, to start work at 9:00 A.M. the next morning.

One of the great joys of doing this book was the wealth of archival material going back to the twenties stored at McMillen Inc. But I would still be wading through it had it not been for Ingrid von Werz, who delved into it with an unerring eye, culled the best from the merely very good, and helped with many of the interviews.

It may seem redundant to say that without Eleanor McMillen Brown (to whom, perhaps I should say, I am not related) this book would not have been possible. But the clarity of her recollections of events that took place sixty and seventy years ago was invaluable.

Betty Sherrill, Ethel Smith, John Drews, and Luis Rey not only submitted themselves to lengthy interviews but never showed any signs of annoyance at my frequent interruptions of their work to check even the smallest point. Their comments and advice have added much to the finished manuscript.

Natalie Davenport, Alexandra Stoddard, Tom Buckley, Ben Flowers, Albert Hadley, Mark Hampton, and Kevin McNamara all talked interestingly—and at length—about their associations with McMillen Inc.

Condé Nast have been very generous in allowing me to use pictures from their archives and, as always, Diana Edkins went out of her way to be helpful.

As its librarian, Margaret Luchar helped me find my way around the files of the Cooper-Hewitt Museum of Design in New York, and Cynthia Olejer transcribed the dozens of taped interviews with great accuracy and patience.

The entire staff of McMillen Inc. were more than cooperative throughout but special thanks go to Irene Booth, Fred Cannon, Terry Gelfand, Mary Louise Guertler, Dale Montgomery, Jimmy Potucek, Peter Robbin and Betsy Shaw.

In London, I owe an unrepayable debt to Marian Underhill and R.W. Apple, Jr., for towing me out of a personal slough of despondency.

As with my previous book, *Interior Views*, I have had the benefit of the acute advice of my editor, Mary Velthoven, and the impeccable art direction of Michael Shroyer. It is a collaboration I have greatly enjoyed.

For Eleanor Stockstrom McMillen Brown

Contents

Preface

The decorative arts are rarely taken seriously enough in this country. Certainly in my own life I have seen the need for good and beautiful design too often ignored, especially by industries devoted to mass production, in which there has often seemed an almost willful lack of respect for aesthetics, whether in the design of automobiles, kitchen appliances, office equipment, or furniture.

In my own career, especially as chairman of Tiffany and Co., I have always believed and promoted the thesis that nothing need ever be ugly or badly designed. We can—and should—be surrounded by beautiful things all through our day-to-day lives. I am therefore more than happy to contribute the preface to a book that shows how this can be—and has been—achieved in a variety of idioms, during more than half a century, by one remarkable woman.

I first met Eleanor McMillen Brown in the mid-1940s, when we both spent summers in Southampton. In fact, I was living in a house she had decorated in the late 1920s for its previous owner. I remember her now as she was then: a serious, down-to-earth woman who believed emphatically in perfection. But there was nothing intimidating in her achievement of this goal. Her own surroundings were always gracious, comfortable, and quietly beautiful—very much, indeed, a reflection of her own personality.

For her clients, she has invariably created the same ambience ever since she started her company, McMillen Inc., in 1924. As times and tastes have changed, so has she, but she has always hewed to the dictum that, whatever its style, nothing that is not truly beautiful has any right to be in a room.

Her educated eye has not only benefited those lucky enough to be McMillen clients; she has also been a strong influence on several generations of decorators and designers, both as a trustee and occasional lecturer at the Parsons School of Design and as the head of the decorating company so many talented young designers have emulated or tried to join. Her reputation is such that Eleanor Brown has always been able to pick from the cream of each new crop of design graduates, and many McMillen alumni have gone on to become well-known decorators in their own right.

It is often said that taste is subjective, but this is only partly true. There is no hard and fast definition of taste, but one is immediately aware of it when it exists and even more acutely aware of it when it is absent. Some people are born with it, some people acquire it, but, alas, it is still true that too many people do not ever possess it. Where good taste exists, it cannot help but give pleasure, as this book illustrates.

I firmly believe that of all the senses, sight is the one most frequently assaulted and insulted today. Some few of us have tried to redress the balance by stressing the importance of beautiful surroundings, whether in the home, in the office, or in public buildings. Eleanor McMillen Brown has been in the forefront of this fight for more than sixty years. Her achievements have been great, and I salute her unwavering pursuit of perfection.

Walter Hoving

Sixty Years of Interior Design

1920

One of McMillen's first public exhibitions was in 1927 at the Exposition of Architecture and Allied Arts in New York. Their booth (*right*) was decorated as a French salon at the time of the restoration of the monarchy (*opposite page*).

In 1924 the United States was invited to participate in what was to prove to be a seminal decorative-arts exhibition: the Exposition Internationale des Arts Décoratifs et Industriels Modernes, to be held the following spring in Paris. President Harding declined the invitation on the grounds that America had no modern decorative and industrial arts.

President Harding was right. In the early 1920s wealthy Americans still aped their European counterparts either by copying ornate French *palais* and sturdy English manor houses or by buying the originals and shipping them, brick by brick, to this country. (One of the most extravagant examples of this kind of procurement and imitation, the vast architectural collage of William Randolph Hearst's San Simeon in California, was completed in 1926.)

Furnishing these houses was done strictly by the period book. A Tudor manor had to be filled with heavy carved oak, its mullioned windows framed by dark velvet curtains. "French" meant either Louis XV or Louis XVI and demanded ornate *boiseries* and moldings and gilded *fauteuils* and *bergères* (usually new reproductions).

The less wealthy—the burgeoning middle class—benefited from the post–World War I building boom but not from the taste of the mass-production Grand Rapids furniture manufacturers, whose output filled many middle-class homes. Stores and mail-order catalogs were still full of prewar golden-oak furniture

(which enjoyed a brief revival a few years ago), and "modern" furniture was typified by "Borax" (short for Bronx Renaissance) pieces, which were elaborate, badly designed and made, and characterized by overstuffed three-piece suites classically covered in taupe mohair.

However, a few pioneering women of good taste—Elsie de Wolfe, Ruby Ross Wood, and Rose Cumming—were letting a few chinks of light into this creatively dark period.

Elsie de Wolfe was born in Brooklyn, lived a great deal in Europe, and exerted her influence in America from the turn of this century until after the Second World War. She was not a creative force: she plagiarized her famous war cry, "Suitability, suitability, suitability," from the novelist Edith Wharton and had no qualms about copying ideas she had seen in France and England. But she was innovative. Although with-

out any formal training, she was the first decorator in the modern sense of the word, and she was the first to stress comfort and use casual chintzes in an otherwise formal room. She encouraged people to discard their heavy Victorian clutter and started the movement toward rooms that were light in both color and content. Her name was made when she was given two major commissions in quick succession—the Colony Club and the second floor of the Henry Frick mansion, both in New York.

Ruby Ross Wood "trained" as a decorator by ghost-writing Elsie de Wolfe's book, *The House in Good Taste*. Then in 1918 she was invited to run America's first department-store decorating service, Au Quatrième, which was about to open in Wanamaker's in New York. Like Elsie de Wolfe, Ruby Ross Wood believed in comfortable, informal, English-style rooms, but her taste at Au Quatrième was more catholic. With Nancy McClelland (who was to write a definitive book on wallpaper), she filled her enclave with French, Italian, and English antiques, rugs, and accessories.

Rose Cumming, an Australian who settled in New York when she was caught there en route to England during the First World War, became a decorator because she "didn't know how to do anything." Frank Crowninshield, the editor of *Vanity Fair*, suggested she try decorating; "First tell me what it is," Miss Cumming replied. She worked briefly at Au Quatrième and then opened her own shop in 1921. A

woman of eclectic—and to some, eccentric—taste, Rose Cumming was to become famous for her use of strong, deep colors such as aubergine, rarely seen elsewhere in the 1920s and 1930s.

These three were women of taste and style, but none of them had formal design training. True, they worked for money, but in the early 1920s, interior design, as it is known today, was not regarded as a profession.

Eleanor McMillen Brown changed all that. It is safe to say that McMillen Inc. was the first professional full-service interior decorating firm in America. When Eleanor McMillen (she became Mrs. Brown in 1934) started her company in November 1924, she was a graduate of the three-year design course at the prestigious New York School of Fine and Applied Arts.

In addition to the creative training, she also possessed a good head for business. "When I decided to go into business, I went to business and secretarial school as well," she says. "I thought if I was going to do it at all, I'd better do it professionally. That's why it's McMillen Inc. and not Eleanor McMillen. I wasn't one of the 'ladies.'"

Like most businesses, it started small, with Eleanor McMillen, financed by $13,000 of her own money and assisted by a secretary, selling furniture from her home, a townhouse at 148 East 55th Street in New York. She had been persuaded to start this venture by William Odom, one of America's leading experts on the decorative arts, who in 1924 was head of the Paris branch of the New York School of Fine and Applied Arts. From this vantage point it was easy for him to cull the best French and English eighteenth-century pieces available in Europe and ship them to McMillen.

"He was a marvelous man with impeccable taste," remembers Eleanor McMillen Brown, who had been one of Odom's favorite students. "It was his idea that he should buy furniture in Europe for me to sell in New York, and at the beginning he had carte blanche. Later on we'd say, 'We're short of chairs' or whatever, and he'd know what to look out for. But we always relied completely on his taste."

William Odom's taste was for the traditional—especially French—and for balance. He had no time for the second-rate. Albert Hadley, a scholar of the decorative arts who has worked at McMillen and is now a partner in the top design firm of Parish-Hadley, says, "Mr. Odom firmly believed that one should not own one single thing that wasn't beautiful. One did not accept a thing simply because it had some romantic association. One simply didn't clutter one's life with an object unless it was beautiful. He preferred to leave a space bare than to fill it with a second-rate object."

William Odom's preference in arranging a room was for precision, but he liked the richness and detail of eighteenth- and early-nineteenth-century French and Italian furniture and he liked elaborate fabrics. The effect of these styles was always controlled in an Odom room by the use of almost austere pale-colored walls.

Eleanor McMillen was not the only person to be influenced by William Odom. As a teacher at, and then as president of, the New York School of Fine and Applied Arts (later to be called the Parsons School after its founder, Frank Alvah Parsons), William Odom had a direct influence on the thinking of three generations of designers and decorators. His opinions continued to be felt long after his death in 1942.

It was by accident as much as design that Eleanor McMillen got to Paris to be taught by William Odom. "I never intended to become a decorator," she says today, almost sixty years later.

Eleanor Stockstrom was born on Feburary 12, 1890, in St. Louis, Missouri. Her father, Louis Stockstrom, who developed the first efficient gas stove, had been born in Germany of Swedish parents. With his brother, he founded the American Stove Company and the two men rapidly built it into the largest manufacturer of gas stoves in America. (Magic Chef is one of their most successful brands.)

So Eleanor Stockstrom was brought up among affluence. There was a townhouse in St. Louis, a country house outside the city, and a summer house in Minnesota. The family—Eleanor had two sisters and a brother—moved among these houses according to the season. Winters were spent in town. In May they moved to the country. August was spent in Minnesota. September found them back in the country house, and at the end of October they returned to the city. It was an ordered, gracious life. "All the houses were kept fully equipped but there were always great caravans of stuff to move with us," she remembers.

Eleanor was educated at Mary Institute, a private school in St. Louis, and went on to Mrs. Knox's Finishing School in Briarcliff, New York. In 1914 she married Drury McMillen, a young engineer also from St. Louis, and they began ten years of peripatetic travel.

Drury McMillen's work took the couple on frequent and extended trips to various parts of South America. Eleanor McMillen found herself in places that had rarely, if ever, seen a white woman before. There were also sojourns in civilization—her son, Louis, was born in Rio de Janeiro in 1916—and between engineering assignments the family would return to a brownstone they had purchased in New York.

It was during these stays in New York that Mrs. McMillen discovered the New York School of Fine and Applied Arts. "It was really the undirected impulse of a young bride wishing for something to occupy her days that got me there," she says. "A school friend was going and she said, 'It's interesting and you've always liked pretty things.' I signed up without knowing what I was doing, and because I was going back and forth to South America, I had to take the three-year course piecemeal."

Piecemeal or not, when she completed her second year the school awarded her an additional year's scholarship for outstanding work. She accepted the honor but, not needing the money, asked that the tuition fees be given to another student. At the end of her third year, she went to Paris for six months to the school's branch in the Place des Vosges run by William Odom.

The main purpose of these six months was to look and learn. Under Odom's tutelage, the students visited most of the great houses and museums in France and Italy. "It was very serious, very good training," Eleanor Brown says now. "It wasn't just decoration. It was art and art history." And, indeed, for the first forty years of its existence, with one exception, only Parsons graduates were hired at McMillen Inc.

In keeping with the period evocation, furniture was arranged in formal, rather stiff groupings such as this one.

European interiors were much in demand in the America of the 1920s. This "French château" in Tuxedo Park mixed periods and styles.

The dining room (*below*) had a *parquet de Versailles* floor, an antique Aubusson rug, and Directoire chairs. The pilasters were designed by McMillen.

The blond paneling in the library was designed by Grace Fakes at McMillen. The rug is another antique Aubusson. The sofa is covered in silk damask, the chair and stool in needlepoint.

Photograph by Emelie Danielson ▶

The Venetian sitting room (*right*) was bought in Europe and shipped intact to New York. The woodwork and dado are white and gold; the walls are hung in silk hand-painted in a chinoiserie pattern.

Photographs by Samuel H. Gottscho

OVERLEAF: The paneling and antique wallpaper panels in the drawing room of the house on page 18 were also shipped from Europe and installed by McMillen.

Designated a "hunting box," Port of Missing Men was the Long Island home of Colonel H. H. Rogers. It was a house of some eccentricity. Each room had its own name. A guest room (*above*) was "The Room of the Mink." The gun room (*opposite*) had a massive vaulted ceiling from which hung a model of a nineteenth-century man-o'-war.

When she graduated, Eleanor McMillen had no thoughts of going into business. She returned to South America with her husband, and it was in Rio de Janeiro that she did her first work. At the request of Edwin Morgan, then ambassador to Brazil, she installed a modern Portuguese interior in the American embassy.

In 1924 she returned to live in New York and started to take herself seriously as a professional.

Elsie Cobb Wilson, a well-known New York decorator, asked Mrs. McMillen to work with her. "I said, 'Oh, I can't work. I've got my husband and child and they take up all my time.' 'Well,' she said, 'just come and you can keep your own hours.'

"I went to work for Elsie and she had William Odom helping her. Elsie was kind of a hot-tempered person, and she and Odom had a good fight one day. He said to me, 'Why don't you let me buy furniture for you this fall and then you can sell it and I'll send you some more?' It all sounded sort of intriguing, and I had finally got settled in my house and got my child to school, so I said I'd do it."

Thus McMillen Inc. was incorporated and a discreet brass plaque was hung outside the door on East 55th Street. Clients came right from the start, mostly friends at first. But as word got around—and Mrs. McMillen wasn't shy of spreading it in her own high social circle—more and more society women visited.

From friends buying the occasional piece of furniture, it was but a short step to their asking McMillen to plan whole rooms and then telling *their* friends when they were pleased with the result. Invariably they were, for Eleanor McMillen's first decorating projects had a lightness and a modernity that were only just beginning to be seen in America.

"Until Eleanor came along," Albert Hadley explains, "the lady decorators were doing pretty, comfy houses without much direction or point of view. It was her strong design consciousness that made McMillen different. She had an educated eye, an educated mind, and she worked relentlessly to achieve perfection and beauty.

"Also, I think Eleanor was ahead of her time in her sense of adventure in bringing things together that were totally compatible but not of the same period. I think it was a return to almost Neo-classical attitudes."

But the company didn't just place furniture and choose fabrics and colors—although Eleanor McMillen's ability to do these things is now legendary. What most set McMillen Inc. apart from other decorators of the day was its ability and willingness to tackle interior architecture as well as decoration.

This advantage came not so much from Eleanor

McMillen herself but from an equally extraordinary woman called Grace Fakes, who had taught at the New York School of Fine and Applied Arts and then gone into business on her own. That venture didn't work. A colleague remembers that Miss Fakes used to say, "I like lions and tigers but not clients."

But Grace Fakes did love—and know—everything there was to know about pilasters, moldings, cornices, *boiseries*, and floor designs of every period—the backbone of interior architecture. In 1926 she joined forces with Mrs. McMillen and remained with the firm until her retirement in the early 1960s.

An early invitation to influential (and wealthy) potential clients described the range of services McMillen Inc. offered. It took the form of a miniature booklet entitled *An 18th-Century Revival*, and stated:

> *McMillen announces the opening of a new shop, novel today but adapted from an 18th-century idea.*
>
> *A complete collection of antique furniture and other decorative objects selected for and ar-*

ranged in every room . . . will allow the client to see each particular thing in its own position, associated with other things with which it is in complete harmony.

Mrs. McMillen is prepared to furnish, in consultation with clients, suggested schemes and drawings for the interior architecture and decoration of simple rooms and complete houses, including remodelling interiors or harmonizing them with adapted period furnishings and decorations.

The 1925 Paris Exposition Internationale des Arts Décoratifs et Industriels Modernes was a watershed in the history of design. For the first time, modernity and the machine were being celebrated for their own sakes, though in radically different ways.

On the one hand was the style that (in reference to the exposition) has become known as Art Deco and that had reached its apogee in 1925. On the other was the school known as the Bauhaus, which was just starting to make its presence felt.

Art Deco had its origins—and its finest flourishing—in France. It began in the years immediately before World War I, and it was, in a way, a reaction against the excesses of Art Nouveau. Art Deco was still luxurious, highly decorative design that demanded the highest-quality craftsmanship. Differently stained woods, ivory, and mother-of-pearl were set into complex floral, abstract, and geometric inlays. Rich woods such as ebony, walnut, and amboyna were used as veneers. Pieces were highly lacquered or covered in snakeskin, shagreen (sharkskin), tortoiseshell, leather, and parchment. Mirror, glass, and chrome were beveled, etched, and lavishly used, and wrought iron became an important decorative element.

But the decorative aspects of Art Deco had a restraint that was lacking in Art Nouveau, and they were always confined within simple, elegant, often Neoclassic shapes. Never, as had been the case with Art Nouveau, was the decorative element allowed to become the form of the furniture. The leading designers were French and included Jacques-Emile Ruhlmann, André Groult, Louis Süe, and André Mare, all of whom had previously been exponents of Art Nouveau.

Most of the rooms had low ceilings and were paneled in the Early American style. Furniture was also Early American and simple—upholstered furniture was slipcovered and hooked rugs were scattered on wide-board floors. One touch of whimsy was the French Provincial wallpaper on one wall of a guest room (*opposite page*).

Whether rustic (*right*), casual
(*above*), or formal (*opposite page*), all
the Americana of Port of Missing
Men was authentic. The furniture
was original, and all the patterned
fabrics antique.

But there was also an avant-garde within this avant-garde movement: Pierre Legrain, who found inspiration in African primitive art, and Eileen Gray, who pioneered luxurious lacquer techniques until the mid-1920s, when she embraced the Modernist movement.

In Germany the Bauhaus, founded in Weimar in 1919 under the leadership of architect Walter Gropius, was hitting full stride. The experimental designs coming from its workshops and formulated for the machine age were revolutionary. The Bauhaus design ethic, summed up in the statement that form should follow function (an expression used in 1880 by American architect Louis Sullivan), produced spare, geometric designs totally devoid of decoration.

By 1925 the Bauhaus had moved to Dessau and shifted its emphasis in furniture design from wood to metal—especially chromium-plated tubular steel—and to standardizing its work for mass production. Leading designers included Marcel Breuer and Mies van der Rohe as well as Walter Gropius. It was in 1925 that Breuer designed his famous tubular-steel and leather "Wassily" chair, named after the painter Wassily Kandinsky, for whose house it was designed. In 1928 came the prototype of the now ubiquitous "Cesca" cane-and-tubular-steel cantilevered chair. (An equally famous chair designed by Mies was to appear at an exhibition in 1929 in Barcelona and take its name from that city.)

It is a paradox, however, that the Bauhaus experiments, meant to make good design economical and therefore available to the masses, were ahead of the available technology. Most of them had to be made—expensively—by hand. It would be another thirty years before machines appeared that could match the precision of man.

The work of the French architect Le Corbusier (never a member of the Bauhaus but always close to it in spirit) was represented at the Paris exposition by the Pavillon de l'Esprit Nouveau.

This early work of the Bauhaus and its continuing influence on architecture and design gave rise to the style known today as International Modernism.

The design revolutions unveiled at the Paris Exposition took a while to cross the Atlantic (America was booming and looking inward, not outward), and when they did arrive it was by courtesy of the department stores, not the furniture manufacturers. By 1927 several stores in New York, the Midwest, and San Francisco had put on view model rooms similar to those shown in Paris in 1925. The public was enthusiastic, and American design caught up with the twentieth century.

OVERLEAF: An early exercise in 1920s "modern." The walls and curtains were pale green, the rug gray. The chairs and sofa were covered in blue-green silk. The metal table had a black glass top, and the mantel was made of mirrored panels.

In the days when boats were yachts, McMillen decorated this one to look more like a seaside home than a home at sea. About the only clues that this room is afloat are the metal hooks battening down the table.

The staterooms were plain but comfortable, and all fabrics were waterproofed to protect against rough weather.

The paneling was pine in the yacht's breakfast area (*above*) and teak in the formal dining room (*right*), where the rug design is a copy of a nautical chart.

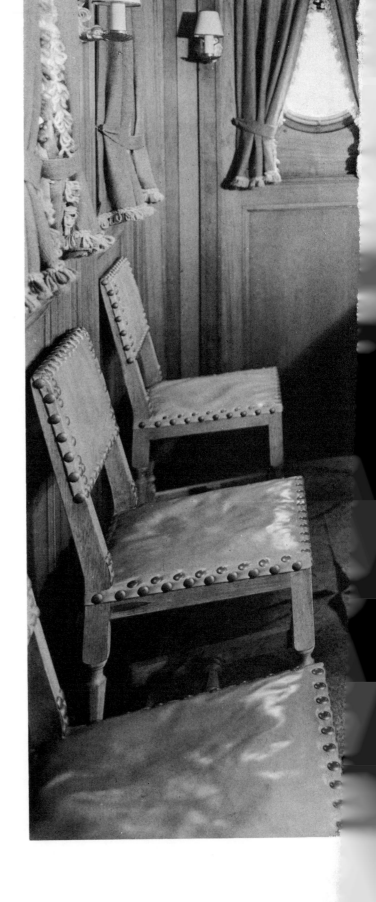

Photographs by Carl Klein Studios

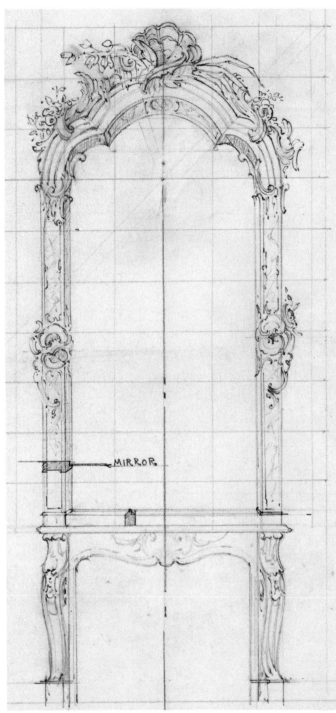

MIRROR

Right from the beginning, McMillen designed and had much of their own furniture and accessories made. These were always meticulously sketched in detail by Grace Fakes. Here, her design for a rococo overmantel mirror.

In the last half of the 1920s, Mrs. McMillen was not working directly in these styles. Like William Odom, and perhaps due to his influence, her taste was classical. Her first love has always been French (especially Louis XVI and Directoire) and English furniture of the eighteenth century. But her concern has always been for background—the architecture of a room—and that didn't have to be of the same period as the furniture as long as it was calm in effect and set the furnishings off to their best advantage.

Her taste was more severe than that of most of her contemporaries and her use of pattern was more restrained. In McMillen interiors, flowered chintzes were rarely used except in country houses—and then they were used sparingly. Wallpaper might be used in bathrooms, dining rooms, and occasionally in bedrooms, but other "public" rooms had plain painted walls defined and relieved by pilasters and by niches that often contained Greco-Roman statuary. Floors were of marble set in classic geometric designs or of handsomely polished wood. Colors were clear rather than deep.

It was not that Mrs. McMillen disapproved of things modern. It was simply that she thought the modern movement had not yet coalesced. In an interview in a 1929 issue of *Country Life*, she said, "I don't think modern has quite reached a complete whole yet. I like the textiles, the glass, some of the ironwork and some of the backgrounds, but the furniture—no." She thought then, as she does now, that its strong lines and uncompromising use of metal were too harsh and uncomfortable-looking. "But," she continued in the same interview, "this year, I'm planning to look at it a little more carefully. So far, I use it cautiously and more in the spirit than in the flesh. Modern treatments, I mean, rather than strictly modern interiors."

And of course few of her clients wanted strictly modern interiors. They were wealthy and had either inherited or were collecting valuable antiques—just the kind of thing William Odom was shipping to McMillen Inc. It was the combination of William Odom's ability to select the best furniture of any period and make it available to McMillen's clientele together with Eleanor McMillen's panache in mixing furniture of different periods against a clean, complementary background that was responsible for much of the firm's early success.

By 1928 business was good enough for Mrs. McMillen to hire Marie Mealand, who remained until the 1940s. She was joined, in 1929, by two more Parsons graduates, Ethel Robertson Smith (who is still with the firm) and Marion Morgan (who retired in 1981). McMillen was getting too big for the ground

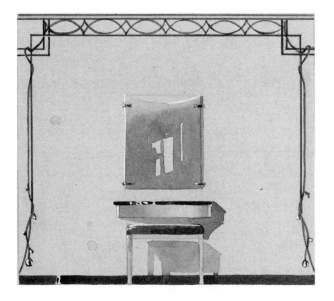
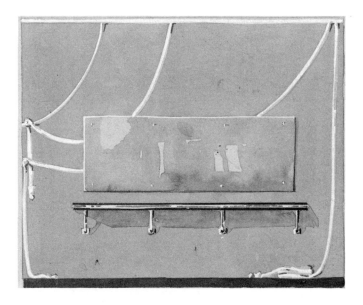
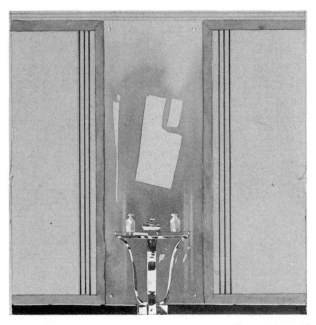

Four watercolor sketches for a high-fashion 1930s dressing room.

floor of the townhouse originally allotted to it.

"It was bedlam and the noise was just awful," Mrs. Smith recalls. "There were about six of us crammed into one room on the ground floor. There was a room at the back of that which was Mrs. McMillen's dining room but also a showroom. The two living rooms on the floor above were also showrooms. Eleanor lived in the rest of the house."

By now, McMillen had clients of the status of Colonel H. H. Rogers, one of the major stockholders of Standard Oil. McMillen furnished his Southampton, Long Island, "hunting box," Port of Missing Men, not only with antique English furniture but also with antique fabrics. "Not even one piece of trimming

was new," Ethel Smith remembers. "Can you imagine that? But we managed to do it." "Colonel Rogers wouldn't come into New York to look at furniture," Mrs. McMillen recalls. "Every piece had to be trucked out to him—a considerable distance in those days. But most of it stayed."

Soon afterward, nineteen-year-old Miss Dorothy Kinnicut married Mr. Henry Parish II, and the bride's mother asked Eleanor McMillen to furnish the couple's Gracie Square house in New York. So it came to pass that it was in a McMillen interior that another doyenne of American interior decorating, second only to Mrs. McMillen herself, the indomitable "Sister" Parish, began her married life.

If appropriate architecture did not already exist, walls and ceilings of McMillen houses were decorated with plasterwork and moldings designed to the desired period by Grace Fakes.

ABOVE AND RIGHT: Neo-classical panels.

TOP AND OPPOSITE PAGE: Carpets were also designed in-house.

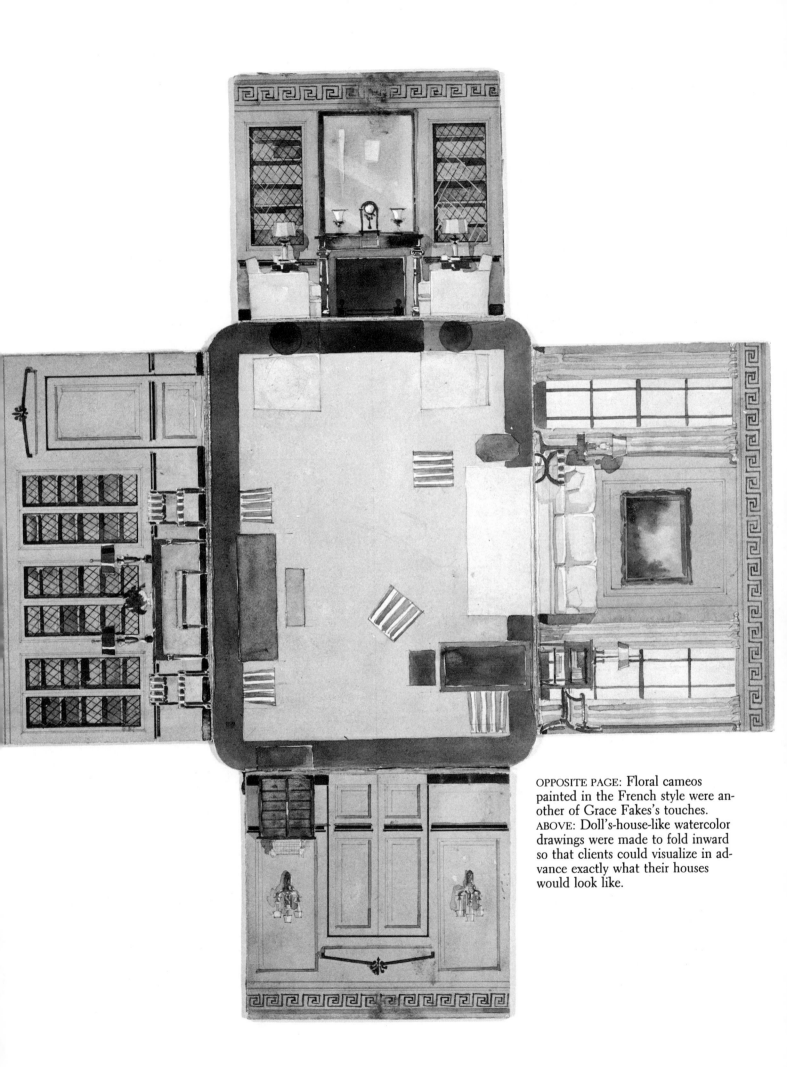

OPPOSITE PAGE: Floral cameos painted in the French style were another of Grace Fakes's touches. ABOVE: Doll's-house-like watercolor drawings were made to fold inward so that clients could visualize in advance exactly what their houses would look like.

Photograph by Drix Duryea

With a group of friends in Southampton in the early 1920s.

Eleanor McMillen in 1932, the year McMillen's model rooms were first displayed throughout the country.

The petite lady sitting by the window of her offices rises to greet a visitor. She is smartly dressed in a tailored blue suit softened by a ruffled silk blouse. Her white hair is impeccably coiffed, her face delicately powdered, and, as she talks, her hands go occasionally to the rope of pearls at her throat. There is a slight frailty in her movements and her voice but great strength and shrewdness in her eyes.

She is talking about how she started McMillen Inc. To hear her tell it, it just grew—from the day in November 1924 when she started selling French furniture from her home to today when its offices two blocks away house a staff of forty-four.

Now, at the age of ninety-two, she is semiretired. But her influence is still felt. She still spends every morning in the office, still casts her sharp eye over the work going on there, and still makes her opinions felt at board meetings.

What made this woman, brought up a lady before working was fashionable and who never *had* to work, such a successful career woman?

Partly it was her innate sense of taste and style—those twin intangibles that form the base for all good interior design. As Eleanor Brown says herself, "I think you have to have a real sense of scale and proportion. You have to have a real feeling for it. I think

A formal portrait taken in the 1950s (*top*) and a family snapshot taken on a golf course showing Eleanor Brown and her second husband, Archibald Manning Brown, flanking two friends.

you are just born with it or you are not. No matter how much training you get, you can't learn that." But she has always combined her creativity with a level head and a pair of feet planted firmly on the ground—characteristics she attributes to her Midwestern upbringing.

It was her levelheadedness that made her realize the importance of running McMillen on sound business principles right from the start. There is no doubt she possesses a good, hard business head, though she says, "I always said, 'Just do excellent jobs and the finances will take care of themselves.' I never worried about a red figure." But she adds, "I had a father who was very money-conscious, and I guess some of that rubbed off on me."

Eleanor Brown is also possessed of a modest ego, and in a profession where egos are rampant, that too aided McMillen's success. She has always derived more satisfaction from building a team than from seeing her own name in lights, and she has a great talent for spotting talent and then treating it well. McMillen has always been prestigious enough to choose from among the best young decorators who in turn have come because of the creative autonomy Eleanor Brown has always allowed them.

No one who has ever known Mrs. Brown dislikes her. She has always been a lady to her fingertips. She has never been heard to lose her temper, though she can be stern. She is reserved but she inspires loyalty. Betty Sherrill, who has been with McMillen for thirty years, has figured out that "Mrs. Brown has kept her staff on average twenty years."

Ethel (Clarke) Smith, who joined McMillen on her graduation from the New York School of Fine and Applied Arts in 1929 and is still with the firm, recalls, "No matter how awful the mistake she'd simply say, 'That's water over the dam.'

"I left in 1938 when my son was born. Seven years later my first husband died, and Mrs. Brown wrote to me as soon as she heard, saying, 'If you're thinking of working again, I hope you'll come back to us.' I lived in Connecticut then, and she said, 'You might find commuting very hard so I just want you to give us whatever time you can. Remember, you don't have to prove yourself. I know you.' She used to watch the clock, and if I had a client and it was getting on to five o'clock, she would come in and say, 'I'm sorry, but Mrs. Clarke has a train to catch and I'll take over for her.' She was so considerate; such a good friend."

Even those who do leave McMillen retain their affection for Mrs. Brown. Albert Hadley says of her: "I arrived in New York from Nashville just after the Second World War. I was looking for a job and, of course, wanted to work at McMillen. I made an appointment with Mrs. Brown. It was the middle of a hot August, and I walked into that glamorous front reception room and there she was, sitting with her back to the window, very trim and chic in a little summer print dress and a navy blue veil pulled over her face and tied up behind. The perfect lady."

But Albert Hadley was not hired. "I hadn't been to Parsons. But I went." After three years as a student and five teaching at the school, Albert Hadley did join McMillen.

John Drews echoes Albert Hadley. "When I arrived for an interview, I was fresh from Parsons. I was scared of this great woman who I had heard about for years. And suddenly, there she was, beautifully groomed. She must have been almost seventy and she looked austere. I was afraid to talk to her, but within fifteen minutes she had me completely at ease and that's one of her great assets. I think that's one of the things that have kept her young and vital: she stayed involved with people and never got above them."

Betty Sherrill says of her: "Basically she's shy and in some ways not an easy person because you can't get close to her. But she and I have been like mother and daughter. We let each other have it like mother and daughter, too."

But to most of the staff, past and present, at McMillen, Eleanor Brown is simply "The Boss." No one can imagine calling her Eleanor. But they tell affectionate anecdotes that span the years.

Of a recent board meeting: "It became so acrimonious. Several of us lost our tempers and were shouting at each other. Finally, Mrs. Brown looked up and said she thought we all ought to meet at her apartment that evening. We did, and in that atmosphere we couldn't yell and scream. Finally everything got sorted out. Mrs. Brown didn't say a word but, at the end, she looked at us all and said, 'Now, did everybody get what they wanted?' "

Of her sprightliness in her old age: "She has always walked up and down steps—in the townhouse, her duplex apartment, at clients' homes. She still does it. Men and women much younger than her would be panting long before Mrs. Brown."

On her personal style: "She's always dressed for dinner. The first time I was invited to her house for dinner, I remember how impressed I was. The maid announced me and there was Mrs. Brown standing by the fireplace wearing a satin gown. I was dressed in a thirty-dollar worn-out jacket. This was when she was in her seventies. She asked if I'd like a martini and then mixed them for us both. I found out later that if you said 'No, thank you,' she'd say, 'Well, I want one,' and go make it."

Another decorator says: "The first time I was in-

At the age of seventy (*above*), Eleanor Brown showed no signs of slowing down. She continued to drive her Thunderbird (*top*) until she was well into her eighties.

Photograph above by Blackstone-Shelburne

43

In a ninetieth-birthday photograph, Eleanor Brown sits in front of the most important piece of furniture in her life: the red lacquer secretary she once lost but found again.

vited to dinner, I told a colleague. 'You will note,' he said, 'that after dinner, she will sit at one corner of the sofa by the door, open the end-table drawer and pull out a little gold compact with a ruby clasp and powder her nose.' And, of course, she did. She is the most methodical person in the world.

"I remember her eightieth-birthday party. I was invited—there were twelve dinner guests. Everyone was bringing presents but I couldn't afford much. I took her a maidenhair fern, I think. Everyone else was giving her diamond earrings and things. It was embarrassing for me, but she just loved it. That's the kind of person she is."

On her relationships with her staff: "She always called us men 'you guys.' But only she could say 'guys' the way she did. She is a very elegant woman who is very down to earth.

"She'd never criticize us in front of clients, but sometimes she'd say after she'd seen a room, 'Don't you think that red's a little harsh, dearie,' or 'That rust was a little too autumnal.' If she really disliked it, she'd have the whole room repainted at McMillen's expense.

"I remember one job going tens of thousands of dollars over estimate and Mrs. Brown saying, 'Boys and girls, we cannot do this.' That's all she said."

On her relationship with clients: "One of the few battles she's ever lost was with Marjorie Merriweather Post. Mrs. Post wanted her ballroom hung in purple. Mrs. Brown hates purple. When Mrs. Post persisted, Mrs. Brown swagged the walls in orchid velvet, hung the windows with plum silk, and, shuddering slightly, left."

Or a more typical outcome of an Eleanor Brown client confrontation: "She didn't want to work for Charles Revson, but she gave him an appointment when he asked her to do the ballroom in his New York apartment. After all, how many opportunities do you get to do ballrooms these days? He arrived on time, she greeted him, and listened to him. Then she said, 'Now, Mr. Revson, I've been told you are very difficult to work with and I love my work and I don't want any problems. If I decide to work with you I want everything to run smoothly.' He just ate out of her hand—I think because everyone else was afraid of him and Mrs. Brown wasn't."

On her ambition: "She loves the word 'success.' If something's good, she calls it a success. When she started, she was determined to be a success. I remember her telling me that when she decided to go into business and told her father in St. Louis, he said, 'But Eleanor, why don't you come home? You can have a business here.' And she said to him, 'I want to be where the rich people are, where I'm at the center of what's going on.' "

So Eleanor Brown stayed in New York at the very center of what was going on. She has devoted her life to building a business that is a success in every sense of the word and, at the same time, found the time to have a successful private life. She has raised a child, himself a successful architect, and is a devoted grandmother. She remained on friendly terms with Drury McMillen, her first husband, after their divorce in 1928 and was then happily married to the architect Archibald Manning Brown from 1934 until his death in 1956.

This level of achievement still eludes the grasp of some of today's career women; it is a sobering thought that this woman had already reached it before most of us were born.

Eleanor Brown, Archibald Manning Brown, and a friend outside Four Fountains, shortly after it was converted from theater to home in the 1940s.

MC MILLEN INC.

The McMillen townhouse at 148 East 55th Street.

RIGHT: A favorite marble bust sat on a gilt console between the living room windows from 1928 until the 1940s, when it was moved to its present position on the mantel.

OPPOSITE PAGE: The hallway of Eleanor Brown's New York duplex apartment has not changed for fifty years. Like all the other decorative elements in the architecture, the balustrade was designed by Mrs. Brown and Grace Fakes.

Photographs by Drix Duryea

To see Eleanor Brown at home is to see her design philosophy at its purest.

McMillen Inc. has worked in every design vernacular during the almost sixty years of its existence but Mrs. Brown herself has stayed faithful to her great loves: Louis XVI furniture and classicism.

Though she shared her townhouse in New York with her company at the beginning, four years later success had driven her to confine her living quarters to the top floor. In 1928 she moved to an apartment near the East River where she still lives. "I was the first and, so far, the only person to live here," she says.

But it's not only her address that has stayed the same through the years. So, in all essentials, has the apartment. The photographs of her dining and living room taken this year are virtually identical with those taken in the 1930s and 1950s.

"Maybe I worked out my own needs for change on my clients," says Mrs. Brown in explanation. "I'm perfectly happy with what I have. It functions and it's very pretty."

Walls have been repainted (the same color every time), furniture has been reupholstered, and some antique pieces added or subtracted over the years but it takes a keen eye to spot the differences. The rooms reflect, as they always have done, the luxury and formality of Mrs. Brown but with a freshness and lightness that is also part of her personality.

Mrs. Brown made architectural changes right at

The living room as it looked in the late 1920s. Changes since then have been subtle (see pages 50–51). The Aubusson rug has given way to several of goatskin, and the console was replaced by a Regency lacquered desk when the marble bust was moved to the mantel. Chairs have also been moved around somewhat.

Photograph by Drix Duryea

the beginning and has never had to rethink them. In the living room, a window was closed off and the walls given definition and symmetry with cornice moldings and pilasters. The dining room was shaped into a flattened oval with four niches. Two walls were mirrored and a large *trumeau* mirror hung over a black marble mantel on another. The walls were painted off-white and a floor designed in green and white marble. White Directoire chairs upholstered in soft butter-colored leather surround an English Regency table. The room remains unchanged.

"The basic rules of proportion and scale are unchanging," Mrs. Brown says. "They are reinterpreted according to the needs of the time. I like simplicity and I believe in restraint. Above all, there should be harmony—of proportion, line, color, and feeling. The most important element in decorating is the relationship between objects—in size, form, texture, color, and meaning. None of these is in good taste in itself but only in relationship to where it has been placed and what purpose it is to serve."

The Neo-classic oval dining room of
Eleanor McMillen Brown's New
York apartment has a green and
white marble floor and leather-
covered French Directoire chairs.

Photograph by Michael Dunne

Mrs. Brown's apartment has remained virtually unchanged during the more than fifty years that she has lived there. As she once said, "If you get it right the first time, there's no need to change." The upholstery is redone and the walls repainted every twenty years or so, but always in the same shades of yellow. Accessories have come and gone, of course, but the design, being classic and timeless, has endured. The same was true of her Southampton, Long Island, house (*shown on the next two pages*), a former theater that she decorated in 1943 and the furnishings of which she sold at Sotheby's when she gave up the house in 1979. Only paint and fabric ever needed rejuvenation. BELOW: The library of the New York apartment changes slightly in summer, when black-and-white slipcovers replace the dark green ones of winter.

The living room has strong Neoclassical overtones. Chairs and sofas are always covered in silk damask. The painting over the sofa (*above, right*) is by Salvador Dali; the red lacquer secretary (*right*) is Venetian.

Photographs by Henry S. Fullerton 3rd

LEFT AND BELOW: Two pictures of the living room taken twenty years apart illustrate its timelessness. The painting of anemones above the sofa is by Raoul Dufy; an English Regency lacquered commode is between the windows.

ABOVE: Elizabeth Hoopes painted renderings of many McMillen interiors. Here, a closeup of the living-room fireplace.

LEFT: The library. The moldings here and in the living room were designed for the flat by Grace Fakes in 1928.

Photographs by Michael Dunne and Tom Yee

ABOVE: Eleanor Brown in the doorway of Four Fountains, the Long Island house she converted from a private theater.

ABOVE RIGHT AND RIGHT: The 40-foot-square living room was divided into several seating areas. The large printed silk toile *Le Cirque* is by Raoul Dufy. The sofas were covered in linen, the Italian rococo chairs in moiré taffeta.

Photographs by Richard Champion

ABOVE: Across the living room from the entrance hall, a low partition hid stairs leading to bedrooms built on the former stage.
LEFT: One bedroom had an old painted Spanish bed and gracefully ethereal window treatment.

Photographs by Richard Champion

In the 1930s McMillen gave the St. Louis house of Mrs. Adolphus Busch a glowing interior.

ABOVE: The living room had an eighteenth-century English marble fireplace, a carved rug, and painted French chairs.

RIGHT: The design genius of Grace Fakes was evident in the bedroom, where she designed the bedhead and canopy, window treatments, and *trompe l'oeil* Italian-style wall panels. The chest is eighteenth-century painted Italian; the end tables twentieth-century, made and painted by McMillen.

BELOW: Mrs. Busch sits beneath her portrait by Bernard Boutet de Monvel.

RIGHT AND ABOVE: In the dining room, Grace Fakes made the modern mantel the dominant decorative feature by surmounting it with an antique plaque and giving it a *faux marbre* surround of her own design. The mirror is Venetian, the console Louis XVI, the rug Aubusson.

ABOVE: The living room of another St. Louis house done in the late 1930s was given walls and wool curtains of an unusual dusky aubergine. The floor was left bare—another unusual feature for that time.

RIGHT: The mirror and crystal glistered and eighteenth-century English furniture gleamed in this New York dining room, decorated in the early 1940s. The painted panels depict scenes of North Africa.

Having got all these elements right in 1928, Mrs. Brown has had no need to change them.

The living-room walls have always been painted yellow ("It's a good city color; it's cheerful"), punctuated by white pilasters. And, because the walls were canvas-lined before the first coat of paint went on, they are washable. They need repainting only every twenty years or so. The Louis XVI chairs have been re-covered in cream and gold damask, but not for eighteen years ("The fabric was Scotchguarded first") and the wood floor was laid in her favorite herringbone pattern. In 1928 it was covered by an Aubusson rug; one major change is that she now uses white goatskin rugs.

There are more subtle changes. The console table between the windows has been replaced by an English Regency lacquered desk and the bust moved to the mantel. There are more chairs and more paintings and, at the far end of the room, one of Mrs. Brown's most cherished additions, an eighteenth-century Venetian red lacquer secretary.

"It came up at an auction in the 1930s," she explains. "I was going out of town, so I put a buy bid on it. When I returned, I phoned to ask how much it had cost me and was told there had been some confusion and it had gone to another bidder.

"About ten years later, I was in a client's house in New Jersey. She told me her mother had given her a lacquer secretary and did I know anything about lacquer. 'I know good lacquer,' I said. She didn't know what to do with it, so it was stored in the basement. I went to look at it and there it was. I made her an offer—remember, I knew how much it had gone for—and bought it. It was meant for me."

She has been just as consistent in the furnishings of her own houses in Southampton. The first was the studio of her second husband, the architect Archibald Manning Brown. What Archibald Brown described as a "rough, camplike workroom" was furnished by his new wife with chenille-covered sofas and pieces from his bachelor apartment in New York.

The color scheme came from the large Raoul Dufy *toile*, *Le Cirque*, with its pink, purple, and blue horses against a yellow-and-brown background. The inside shutters were pink, the curved sofa yellow, the Italian chairs painted gray-green, all set against white walls and ceiling.

Unfortunately, this studio was on the Southampton dunes and did not survive the hurricane that attacked Long Island in 1938, though many of the furnishings did. After the hurricane, the Browns rented houses for a few summers until, in 1942, they bought the house that Mrs. Brown kept until 1978.

An early view of Mrs. Brown's dining room.

OVERLEAF: After her marriage to the architect Archibald Manning Brown, Eleanor Brown moved into his studio on the dunes in Southampton. The studio's proximity to the sea proved to be its downfall; it was destroyed in the 1938 hurricane that hit Long Island.

Photograph by Samuel H. Gottscho

OVERLEAF: Archibald Brown credited
his wife with transforming his
"rough, camplike workroom" into a
comfortable home. The shutters,
painted pink, were set off by white
walls; the curved chenille-covered
sofa was yellow; and the Italian chairs
were painted gray-green.

The opposite wall of the living room was paneled with bookshelves. Between them is the painting *The Accordion Player* by William L'Engle.

The color scheme for the studio came from the large Raoul Dufy *toile Le Cirque*, with its pink, purple, and blue horses.

Photographs by Samuel H. Gottscho

Four Fountains, as it was called, has its own history. Archibald Manning Brown had designed the building, along with a huge estate of which it was the private theater, in 1930. But by 1942 it was too much for the owner to keep up and the Browns bought the theater along with a little land.

Eleanor Brown set to work to transform this pavilion—a unique example of American Art Deco expressed in classic form—into a private summer house that would be elegant and comfortable.

The auditorium (which measured 40 by 40 feet with 20-foot-high ceilings) became a huge multipurpose living room. The scale was grand and dramatic but, thanks to Eleanor Brown's gift for flexible seating arrangements, the setting she created was intimate.

"I liked to entertain in small groups. More than four people had to be able to converse together, yet two be able to talk together privately and one able to sit and read without feeling lonely. Nothing is worse than having to sit with a not-particular friend on a loveseat barely made for two or be separated at far corners of the living room when less formality would be better."

"Nobody arranges furniture as well as Eleanor Brown," her fellow designers admit, and she arranged this huge room to offer all the options she wanted without frequently having to move furniture about.

There were basic seating units of a sofa and two comfortable chairs, each with nearby benches and straight-backed chairs that could be pulled up to join the grouping when wanted. The addition of a fireplace and two windows at one end of the room made natural focal points. Tables held objects and served as free-standing partitions and one end of the living room was given over to a dining area.

Other major architectural changes were made right at the beginning. The raised stage was redesigned to make two double bedrooms and bathrooms. A church organ was removed and guest rooms were built over the foyer in what had been the projection room.

Like the New York apartment, once Four Fountains was finished it changed very little during the more than thirty-five years Mrs. Brown lived there.

Furnishings salvaged from the studio, including the Dufy *toile*, were joined by "things we had accumulated"—again mostly French eighteenth-century furniture with some Italian pieces. And during those years, Mrs. Brown re-covered the sofas and chairs precisely once—and in exactly the same colors as before.

In 1978 the house was sold to William Paley, chairman of CBS, and in March 1979 Mrs. Brown sat in the balcony at Sotheby Parke Bernet and watched its contents go under the hammer. At the end, a standing-room-only gallery, which included just about every decorator in New York, had spent $198,965.

Yes, Mrs. Brown said, she had regrets about selling, but "it had just become too much of a burden for me. I mean, I'm really old. Well, I'm eighty-nine years old. I think that's perfectly old."

After the hurricane, the Browns managed to salvage some of the furniture, including this pair of Italian *fauteuils*.

Photograph by Samuel H. Gottscho

Four Fountains had been designed by
Archibald Brown as a private theater
in the late 1930s. When the opportunity arose, the Browns bought it and
turned it into their summer home
(see pages 52–53).

68

OPPOSITE PAGE: Four-poster beds were designed in all shapes and styles. TOP: An antique Chinese wallpaper was planned for a dining room and (*above*) the furnishings for a living room were detailed right down to the miniaturized copy of the painting that would hang over the mantel.

RIGHT AND OPPOSITE PAGE: In 1946 McMillen turned its townhouse back into a "private" house to sell William Odom's furniture and *objets*. The mirror is Empire, the chaise Regency.

William McDougall Odom was born in Columbus, Georgia, in 1886. A fall from his horse when he was five left him an invalid until he was ten. His first love was music and his father sent him to New York to study under Leopold Stokowski, then organist of Saint Bartholomew's Church in Manhattan. But Stokowski, fearing that Odom's health would not stand up to the rigors of the life of a professional musician, advised him to take a course in commercial art.

So Odom went to the New York School of Fine and Applied Arts and studied interior decoration. He graduated in 1908 and returned to teach at the school in the following year. In 1920 he founded the Paris branch of the school.

In 1930 Odom became president of the school though he continued to live in Paris with frequent visits to Italy. There was not a palace, manor house, or museum in either country that he did not know inside and out and he shared his knowledge with his students. William Odom believed that good modern design depended on a thorough knowledge of the past.

"He was an odd kind of person in some ways," Eleanor Brown says. "He was rather shy but very socially minded. He liked people who represented society. He lived very extravagantly with a beautiful car and chauffeur. Of course, in those days that wasn't such an extravagance as it would be today. But he was really extraordinary. He couldn't put a book down on a table in a way that didn't look special."

A magnificent Regency breakfront spanned one wall. It was 15 feet wide and 10½ feet high. The round table is Directoire.

William Odom collected beautiful furniture for himself as well as for McMillen. In 1939, planning to retire, he moved to London. When the blitz started, he moved his belongings to the country—presciently as it turned out, for not long afterward a direct hit by a bomb destroyed his London house.

Odom died in 1942 and his furniture remained in England until after the war. In 1946 his sister, who had inherited his estate, asked Mrs. Brown what she should do with the furniture. "She couldn't use it, so we decided that it would all be put on sale at McMillen. She said she'd give 10 percent of the sale to Parsons School and that interested me. So we used our rooms in the townhouse and painted and decorated them to look like a private house again and we furnished them with his things.

"He had such beautiful things—everybody who had heard of Odom knew what his taste was—and the first day, we sold something like 80 percent of what was there. People just flocked."

Two unusual bookcases: The tall, gracefully proportioned mahogany cabinet (*above*) dates to the Directoire period but looks English in its severe simplicity. With its intricate decoration, the black-and-gold lacquer bookcase (*right*) looks French, but it is in fact English Regency.

Photograph at right by Ernemac Photo Service

ABOVE AND ABOVE RIGHT: William Odom collected period objects eclectically but each piece was chosen with a precise eye. Symmetry was everything in his arrangements. In the vignette (*right*) are one of a pair of Regency bronze-and-marble lamps, one of a pair of alabaster-and-ormolu vases, a French Empire box with ormolu mounts and Sèvres insets, and a Louis Philippe perfume bottle.

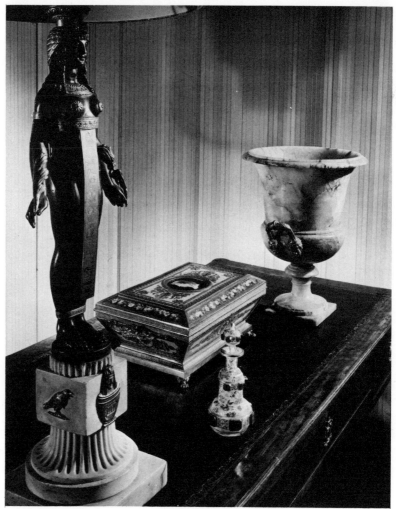

*Photographs above and right
by Hans van Nes*

A collection of Piranesi drawings was hung in one bedroom (*above left*), while groupings of nineteenth-century watercolors and Neo-classical drawings were put in another (*left*). The dining table (*above*) was set with Italian crystal and French porcelain. The Neo-classicism Odom loved was represented (*opposite page*) by the urn on a *faux marbre* pedestal, the candelabra, and the painted Italian table.

1930

RIGHT AND OPPOSITE PAGE: For a chic ladies' dress shop in St. Louis, McMillen produced an essay in severe Neo-classicism with Art Deco touches.

By 1930 the staff at McMillen—decorators, assistants, secretaries, shipping clerks, and bookkeepers—numbered twenty-five, and Eleanor McMillen had divorced her husband, moving out of the townhouse into the apartment on East 57th Street where she still lives.

But then came the Depression and difficult years for everyone, including McMillen Inc.

The wealthy clients on whom decorators depend disappeared overnight—as had their fortunes in many cases. And for those who did not go under, the thought of spending, especially on decoration, was the furthest thing from their minds.

Many decorators had a staff of one and so had only themselves to consider. But Eleanor McMillen was not in that position. It was her early success and prudent business management that enabled her—and her company—to survive.

She remembers the Depression as being tough but not tough enough to frighten her. Dipping into the firm's capital (and perhaps her own) she managed to keep her staff on, although Ethel Smith says, "Every month our salaries were lowered, so we ended up practically working for peanuts. But so was everyone else. You were lucky just to have a job. So we struggled along."

Today Eleanor Brown dismisses that period as a mere punctuation mark. "We had had no experience with a depression, so at first we didn't know how to

Decorated in the 1930s, the shop looked like a high-fashion, if formal, apartment—a design that suited the high-fashion, formal clothes it stocked behind closet doors.

handle it. But the overhead wasn't so high that we couldn't carry it. Fortunately, we were able to see ourselves through and come out of it."

As the country recovered, so did McMillen—and rapidly. Private clients returned, and the company found itself doing its first contract work—for the Cosmopolitan Club and for the Steuben Glass showroom, both in New York.

By 1933 the country and the design world had recovered sufficiently to stage a "Century of Progress" exposition in Chicago. The row of model homes at this exposition—and especially "the house of the future"—was the first exposure to modern architecture and design for tens of thousands of Americans.

This Streamlined Moderne, as it came to be called, was an American style that had evolved from both the Art Deco and the Bauhaus designs of the 1920s; it probably would have made an earlier and deeper impression on American taste had it not been for the Depression. But after 1933, perhaps because the social and economic shocks of the previous few years had destroyed most people's faith in institutions and the status quo, it found a ready acceptance.

Streamlined Moderne was high style, pioneered by industrial designers such as Raymond Loewy and Norman Bel Geddes, and it reached its zenith in the design of the transcontinental trains and transatlantic liners of the day. It was, Philippe Garner says in his book *Twentieth-Century Furniture*, "a style based on a fantasy vision of a world of easy travel and mechanised living uncluttered with references to the past and itself a dream image for the future."

Furniture was low, horizontal, and simply shaped, based on the fundamental forms of architecture—the rectangle, the triangle, and the circle. Lines were sleek and the big free-flowing curve became important. Ornament became superfluous, and floor space was cleared by the introduction of the first multipurpose wall units, which combined bookshelves, cabinets, and desks.

Metal—brass, chrome, and aluminum—superseded wood, though cabinetmakers fought back with new veneers—light woods were left light or dark ones bleached—to keep up with the times. The first glass-topped tables appeared, and both clear and smoked mirror glass were used to panel walls and as an alternative furniture veneer.

With so many reflective surfaces being used, it wasn't just the shape of the furniture that had to be simple. Color had to be clear and pale, and pattern, where it existed, abstract.

Streamlined Moderne got another push at a 1934 exhibition at New York's Metropolitan Museum of Art. Here were rooms by Eliel Saarinen and Raymond

Pride of place in a bedroom setting designed for the Golden Gate Exposition of 1939 went to this mirrored dressing table decorated with astrological symbols.

OVERLEAF: Also in the 1930s, McMillen produced high-style designs for Millicent Rogers, a noted beauty and the daughter of Colonel H. H. Rogers, for whom they had created interiors emphasizing Americana in the 1920s.

Photograph by Hans van Nes

Loewy, and one by the architect Archibald Manning Brown, who had recently married Eleanor McMillen.

Then at the end of the decade came the 1939 New York World's Fair. Here the section "Building the World of Tomorrow" was seen by millions. The new furnishings were shown in their best surroundings; in the new streamlined architecture based on the new building materials—steel, glass, and reinforced concrete.

Streamlined Moderne had an impact that is still being felt today—indeed, it is being revived—but who knows how much stronger it might have been had war not turned everyone's thoughts away from tomorrow to concentrate on surviving today?

As it was, Streamlined Moderne had its problems. This was high-style, and its price was high. For although this modern furniture was designed for the mass market, it suffered, as did the Bauhaus designs, from the fact that it was ahead of technology and that the very simplicity of its design—any mistake became glaring—demanded the quality finish that could only be produced by hand. And that was expensive. As such, it was always outside the range of the average American's purse, and what cheap versions did come off the assembly lines looked every bit as badly made and badly finished as they inevitably were.

Also, even for the wealthy, this was a very demanding style. All those pale colors and shiny surfaces had to be kept exceptionally clean; the slightest mark marred their perfection.

By the last half of the 1930s a growing rebellion against the high cost and stylistic demands of Streamlined Moderne had led to another decorating style—Eclecticism—that continues up to today.

Modernism in America was essentially the vernacular of architects. Decorators, who were now proliferating and being taken seriously as professionals, throughout the decade favored a much more romantic look, one that had its roots in tradition. The Neo-classical style continued, but now it was joined by Neo-baroque and Directoire-modern.

Neo-baroque found its staunchest fans in Hollywood and in an entertainment world that sought the trappings of glamour. Sofas and chairs were covered in shining satin and were tufted, stitched, piped, and buttoned. Walls were covered in padded, quilted satin.

The entrance hall had a classic black-and-white checkerboard marble floor and a tufted satin sofa. The curved ceiling was painted to simulate fabric that ended in a *trompe l'oeil* tasseled pelmet.

Photograph by André Kertész

OVERLEAF: A contemporary room in 1938 had many aspects considered contemporary today: a high-gloss tiled floor, leather-covered furniture, and a fig tree.

Photograph by Samuel H. Gottscho

The living room was swagged in crimson silk, the furniture was upholstered in silk, satin, and velvet, and an antique needlepoint rug brought a strong pattern into the room.

Photograph by Hans van Nes

Photograph by Gottscho-Schleisner

Another view of the room illustrated
on the previous page. The murals of
a modern-dress Don Quixote are by
Jan Juta.

Windows were elaborately curtained and ornate crystal
chandeliers dripped from ceilings. Syrie Maugham, the
wife of the author Somerset Maugham, imported her
own elegantly pared-down version of this style when
she arrived from England in 1934 to do her already
famous all-white rooms in America.

Directoire-modern became popular with those
who admired the elegant lines of the new furniture but
not its stark functionalism. Directoire dates from the
period from 1795 to 1804 in France—when the Di-
rectory ruled after the revolution, before Napoleon
crowned himself emperor. The style was an extension
into the realm of design of the admiration of the
French revolutionaries for the ideas of the ancient re-
publics of Greece and Rome. A lot of Directoire furniture was still based on Louis XVI designs, but these
were simplified and made more severe; other pieces
copied more exactly the classic Greco-Roman shapes
and motifs—scrolls and keys, bas-relief figures, urns,
and lyres. The Directoire style bridges Louis XVI and
Empire. But while it uses decorative elements as liber-

ally as either its predecessor or successor, Directoire
uses them with calculated control.

There were also pockets of the surreal and fanciful.
In France, Salvador Dali was designing such furniture
as his "Mae West's lips" sofa, and Alberto Giacometti
and his brother Diego were making their stick-thin
bronze tables and chairs. The work of both Dali and
the Giacomettis was used by one of the most famous
French furniture and interior designers, Jean-Michel
Frank. Frank had moved away from his early soft and
subtle modernism, which used natural materials in
their natural colors, into a more fanciful mood. It was
a mood soon imported to America, especially to the
West Coast, by more avant-garde decorators, such as
Frances Elkins.

Frances Elkins also helped foster a growing interest in contemporary American craftsmanship, as did
Rose Cumming and "Sister" Parish in New York.
"Sister" Parish was just starting a career that would
make her name a byword for ease, comfort, and the
undecorated "English country house" look.

Another important influence for the future made
itself felt at the 1937 International Exposition of Arts
and Techniques in Paris, and then again in 1939 in
the Finnish Pavilion at the New York World's Fair.

This was the work of Alvar Aalto. Aalto, a Finn, espoused the basic design premises of the modernists such as the cantilever chair, but eschewed the use of metal.

Instead, he used blond wood—very often birch—developing a method of laminating strips of wood into a plywood that had the strength and resilience of tubular steel. World War II delayed the impact in America of Aalto and his fellow Scandinavians so that it was not until the 1950s that their influence was really felt.

With or without a Second World War, however, these new styles were so different from anything ever seen before that they would probably have taken time to become popular. The new designs in furniture and architecture had certainly gained a foothold, but most Americans were still deeply conservative. A 1937 poll taken by one architectural magazine discovered that 85 percent of the people able to buy homes in the middle-cost bracket (which was $10,000 at that time) still preferred the Colonial style.

Country French was the style in the music room of the Connecticut home of Mr. and Mrs. Hubert McDonnell. The walls were gray, and the furniture was upholstered in green. The moldings and plasterwork were designed by Grace Fakes at McMillen.

Photograph by Carl Klein Studios

The McDonnell living room (*above*)
had greater formality, but retained a
country freshness.

The dining room (*right*) was simply furnished so that nothing would distract from the magnificent red-and-cream antique Aubusson rug.

Luxury was the key in the master bathroom (*right*), with its *faux marbre* walls and extravagantly trimmed curtains. It boasted an Aubusson rug and French antiques.

Photograph by Carl Klein Studios

OVERLEAF: A pine-paneled library of another 1930s house was furnished with traditional but comfortable furniture and decorated with family memorabilia.

ABOVE: The drawing room was also furnished in a traditional style but with greater formality. The delicate tracery of the mirror's frame is a McMillen design.

OPPOSITE PAGE: A narrow hallway gains an effect of greater width from the diagonal placement of the floor tiles.

Photograph by Samuel H. Gottscho

By the time of the 1933 Chicago exposition the economy was recovering, and private clients, old and new, flocked through the doors of McMillen Inc. The company consolidated and expanded. Throughout the 1930s Eleanor McMillen Brown also taught at the Parsons School, traveled to Europe on buying trips every year, and, increasingly, traveled in America on McMillen commissions.

She returned frequently to her hometown of St. Louis, where she worked on houses for Mrs. James Bush and for Mrs. Adolphus Busch (of the Anheuser-Busch brewing family), among others.

Many of the firm's New York clients bought winter homes in Florida, so there was work to be done in Palm Beach. And in and around New York, there were enormous houses and apartments to be done for such leading families as the Marshall Fields and the McDonnells.

Mr. and Mrs. James McDonnell had fourteen children, an enormous duplex in Manhattan, and a house in Southampton. McMillen's work for the McDonnells led to one of their daughters becoming a client—when she became Mrs. Henry Ford II and, later, as Mrs. Deane Johnson—and inspired commissions from their other children as well.

HERE AND ON THE NEXT THREE
PAGES: Two libraries, two drawing
rooms, and two dining rooms from
two houses, each with a comparable
layout and each decorated with tradition firmly in mind. Both houses had
formal furniture that was formally
placed, but the first had a compara-
tively casual scheme, while the second was definitely high-style.

Photograph by Samuel H. Gottscho

Photographs by Hans van Nes

A classic essay in decorating with
Fine French Furniture, the epitome
of *luxe* before the Second World
War. Backgrounds were also fine and
French, with antique paneling in the
library (*opposite page*) and antique
wallpaper panels in the master bedroom (*top and above*) and a guest
room (*left*).

Contemporary (1930s) and traditional were mixed in this architecturally classical loggia. Chairs and sofa were covered in chenille.

Photographs by Samuel H. Gottscho

The dining room was more strikingly modern, with its clean lines broken only by the curves of the nineteenth-century painted chairs.

One of McMillen's first contract jobs was the decoration of the Cosmopolitan Club in New York when the club moved into its new building (*right*) in 1933. McMillen worked with its architect, Thomas Harlan Ellett, from the start. The entrance hall (*above*) had a black, gray, and white floor and a dark aubergine domed ceiling from which hung a reproduction of a Russian lantern. The reading room (*opposite page*) was wood-paneled by the architect and decorated in shades of terra-cotta and pine green by McMillen. The seating came from the old club and was slip-covered.

Photographs by Samuel H. Gottscho

The architectural detailing of the ballroom was installed by Thomas Harlan Ellett. McMillen put mirrors on one wall and *trompe l'oeil* silk curtains on another.

The dining room had the same black, gray, and white floor as the entrance hall. The walls were painted lemon yellow, the curtains were white linen with yellow-and-green trim, and the dining chair seats were green. The wall lights (*below*) were designed by Grace Fakes.

HERE AND ON THE NEXT TWO PAGES: Another early contract commission was the redesign of the Steuben Glass showroom in New York. With its almost Minimalist all-white walls, Art Deco details, and clean, sweeping lines of fixtures, it looks very much of today. It was done in the early 1930s.

Photograph by Rotan

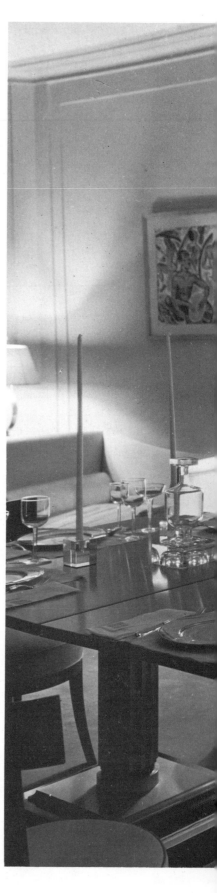

111

Because of Eleanor Brown's firm belief that architecture comes before decoration, McMillen never seems to have had the problems in working with architects that still, today, are the bane of many decorators' lives. (Architects will reverse that sentence.)

In an article written in 1931 for the magazine *Interior Architecture and Decoration,* Mrs. Brown explains her company's success in this still-fraught-with-friction relationship. "Architects who feel that the decorator often fails to complement the character of the building . . . [are recalling] a flimsy shadow of the past who used to pose as a decorator when he was really nothing more than an arranger of furniture.

"[McMillen] offers the architect a readable design of the finished room with sufficient sketches, floor plans, material and color samples to settle all doubt at the beginning [about] what the completed rooms would be.

"It is to the client's advantage and also the architect's, to have a trained and experienced decorator with both technical knowledge and an understanding of interior architectural detail so as to be able to assemble intelligently the proper textures, colors, furniture and objects to make a consistent room. If all these things are taken into consideration in the original planning . . . a great many difficulties can be anticipated."

Two clients who took this advantage during the 1930s were the builders of the new Cornell Medical Center, who asked McMillen to consult with the architects on the colors and furnishings for patients' rooms, and property developers Douglas Elliman, who came to McMillen for advice on how to remodel out-of-date apartment buildings. Both were high compliments for a still-youthful company in a still-young profession.

Work still came spontaneously via word of mouth—although some of Mrs. Brown's friends were offered, and were paid, a commission for any friends they steered to McMillen as clients.

And one thing led to another. As a result of decorating the home of Arthur Houghton, the owner of Corning Glass, McMillen received a commission in 1934 to remodel the Steuben Glass showroom in New York. From clients who were members and on its board came a commission in 1933 to renovate the Cosmopolitan Club.

By the mid-1930s Mrs. Brown had hired Martha Snyder, who was to run McMillen's expanding business office with an iron hand for more than thirty years, and her decorating staff of Grace Fakes, Marion Morgan, and Ethel Smith had grown to include Sam Hughes, who was to remain with McMillen for over twenty-five years, and Natalie Davenport, who is still associated with the company.

Sam Hughes, who trained as an architect but never took his degree, was another Parsons School of Design graduate. He joined McMillen's design department as Grace Fakes's assistant and provided help that by now she badly needed.

Natalie Davenport was the first—and for many years the only—nongraduate of Parsons to work at McMillen. Mrs. Brown made the exception "because Natalie, like her mother, who was a great friend of mine, had great personal style and I knew she had been brought up to appreciate beauty." Natalie Davenport's flair for the new and different (which comes, she says, "from vanity: I always wanted to experiment and do things that had never been done before") soon became an important ingredient in McMillen's versatility.

Another important designer who came to McMillen in this decade was Zalina Comegys Brunschwig. She remained until the beginning of World War II, when she became head of the fabric firm of Brunschwig & Fils after her husband, Colonel Roger Brunschwig, went back into military service.

This expanded team did all kinds of work— English for the McDonnells, French and Italian for the Buschs, high-style Neo-classical for Millicent Rogers (a leading beauty and the daughter of Colonel H. H. Rogers, for whom McMillen had done Port of Missing Men in the 1920s), and the Steuben showroom.

McMillen, though it was always up-to-date, did not do too much work in the modern vernacular. Eleanor Brown has never espoused the use of the harder edges of functionalism. She recently reiterated her belief, much as she had expressed it in 1964 in *The Finest Rooms by America's Great Decorators*, edited by Katharine Tweed, that "there is nothing more trite than a set period—any antique period bought intact for today's living. But, by the same token, a contemporary house that ignores all vestiges of the past in order to express a purely modern philosophy runs the risk of becoming a stagnant document of its own time.

"Taste is relative, but to be positive and vital it must respect the past, accept the present and look forward with enthusiasm to the future.

"The contemporary eye combines objects and materials of the present with objects and materials from the past, not because of fashion but because of one's own knowledgeable eclecticism—the result of one's own varied experiences and cultivated taste.

"Contemporary paintings and sculpture are happy with furniture of the past. Fabrics of contemporary colors and textures are suitable and appealing on old chairs. Old patterns seem excitingly fresh when rejuvenated by a contemporary palette. Modern lighting and ventilation enhance otherwise traditional rooms. The settled, comfortable look of beautiful upholstery makes otherwise austere rooms more cozy and adds to rooms of clinical structure the traditional qualities of charm and comfort. Active, positive taste demands a constantly fresh appraisal of familiar forms—holding on to those things that add quality, beauty, and pleasure to one's life, disposing of superficial impediments."

There was no lack of wealthy clients who agreed with this philosophy of Mrs. Brown's; these were people who could afford quality but who lacked her fine editor's eye for what worked together and what didn't.

And Mrs. Brown did not hide her light under a bushel. Throughout the 1930s, McMillen mounted a series of educational displays in the townhouse. "Crystal Mirrors of the XVIII and XIX Centuries," "Painted Italian Furniture of the XVIII Century," "18th-Century Drawings" all drew people—each one a potential client—to the showroom. McMillen also did a room setting for a Fine Arts Exhibition at Rockefeller Center in New York in 1935 and one at the Golden Gate Exposition in San Francisco in 1939.

Mrs. Brown wrote articles for decorating magazines on such subjects as Directoire rooms, decoration during the Regency, future trends in decoration, the profession of interior decoration and, of course, the work of McMillen Inc. This work was also displayed in room settings designed for magazines, in small advertisements, and in window dressing for such stores as Bonwit Teller and Lord & Taylor.

For all her wealthy clientele, Mrs. Brown was not interested in the kind of exclusivity that demands anonymity in the world at large. Indeed, she was delighted when *American Home* magazine asked McMillen to decorate a house with furnishings the average reader could afford—and could find in the stores.

So by the end of the decade McMillen was not only one of the most prestigious decorating firms in America, it was also the best known.

HERE AND OVERLEAF: Two views of
the library designed by Eleanor
McMillen Brown for clients in the
1930s. Their eldest son now lives in
the house and is also a client of
McMillen's. To see the subtle
changes the room has undergone
since then, see page 143.

McMillen decorated the drawing
room with chinoiserie wallpaper
panels for the father. For the son,
McMillen moved the panels to the
dining room and installed wood paneling throughout (see pages 142–44).

Photographs by Hans van Nes

Some of the McMillen staff at work on the miniature rooms.

McMillen Inc. survived the Depression partly because of Eleanor Brown's determination not to dismiss any of her staff, whether decorator or shipping clerk. "It wasn't just that we were looking for some way to keep our people," she says today, "though we were. We had a good staff and a big investment in them.

"But nothing is more ruinous to morale than having nothing to do, and I did not want to see anyone on the staff undergoing a heartbreaking siege of idleness. Then Grace Fakes came up with the idea of making miniature rooms and exhibiting them.

"I thought that sounded sort of interesting but I didn't have a clue how to make them. Grace said, 'Don't bother, I know how. If you take care of the publicity and launching, I'll see they are designed and made.' I had no idea what we had started."

What they had started was to become one of the most intriguing and successful traveling design exhibitions of all time.

Under Grace Fakes's design direction, the staff were set to building and making the furniture for a series of nine rooms. Each was scaled at one and a half inches to a foot and the largest was three feet long. All were furnished down to the last detail.

"It was an attempt to take a peep into the future," Mrs. Brown commented at the time. "But the rooms are modern interpretations of the classic and stress the importance of proportion and composition. They are not intended to be radical in any respect."

But they were radical in their very existence. The detail was extraordinary. The scaled-down copies of

Eleanor McMillen at the opening of "Interiors of Tomorrow," her exhibition of miniature rooms. On her right is the muralist Jan Juta, on her left the sculptor Wheeler Williams, both of whom worked on the project.

Three views of the penthouse sun-
room, with its mirrored walls and
ceiling, tiny real plants, and murals
by Barry Faulkner.

ABOVE, THIS AND OPPOSITE PAGE:
Two views of the blue-and-white bedroom. With its miniature magazines
and memorabilia, it is complete in
every detail.

RIGHT: The black-and-white library,
with busts by Wheeler Williams and
a painted panel by Van Day Truex.

LEFT: An entrance hall had a terrazzo floor and paintings on glass by Jan Juta.

ABOVE AND RIGHT: A skyscraper office was designed by Victor Proetz. There was even an accurately scaled down typewriter. The books were all bound in vellum and stamped in gold.

Photographs by Emelie Danielson

OPPOSITE PAGE: The true-to-life copy of Mrs. Marshall Field's living room.

Aubusson rugs, marble floors and fireplaces, and crystal chandeliers were all real. Each tiny piece of furniture was made in exactly the same way as a full-sized piece. Sculptors re-created their work in miniature and painters their portraits. Every piece in every room was made especially for its setting, including miniature magazines, books, cigarettes, thermos bottles, a typewriter and desk accessories.

The architectural detailing was so good that a picture of one room ran in the May 1932 issue of *Town and Country* magazine without anyone realizing it was not a full-sized room.

The dining room, Mrs. Brown's favorite and not unlike the one in her own New York apartment, was octagonal. Walls were painted white with a blue domed ceiling and blue niches. Niches and ceiling were indirectly lit by tiny bulbs. The floor was a geometric design in gray, white, and black marble. Busts on plinths were original studies by the sculptor Wheeler Williams. White lacquered chairs upholstered in white kid were pulled up to a glass-topped round table. Two side walls were mirrored and another was taken up by a doorway that opened onto a garden.

A circular library had black lacquer walls with white carpeting and a domed ceiling. Furniture was upholstered in white silk and green leather. All the books were bound in white vellum tooled with gold and over the mantel hung a miniature painting by Jan Juta.

In the eighteenth-century drawing room, a replica of a real room designed for Mrs. Marshall Field, all is as it was in real life. Aubusson rug, chandelier, Regency furniture, andirons, and Chinese porcelain are scaled down from originals and Bernard Boutet de Monvel, a noted portrait painter, made a miniature of his real portrait of Mrs. Field.

Blue-and-white-striped taffeta on a chaise and chairs, white carpeting, and a glass-and-mirror bed and dressing table made a cool but feminine bedroom. The architectural detailing of moldings and convex walls was immaculate, as was the copy of a Matisse hanging on one wall.

A skyscraper office (the Empire State Building was opened the same year that these models were made) was the last thing in business chic. The room and its furniture were the conception of the independent designer Victor Proetz. It had brown walls, black leather chairs, and a couch and lounge chair covered in red leather. Nothing very revolutionary there, but one contemporary newspaper account mentions "its large corner windows—a recent development in skyscraper architecture" and now, of course, coveted by

1888

1833

1860

the status- and power-hungry. Another newspaper described the novel window treatment: "The drapes themselves are of metal; that is, they apply vertically the principle used horizontally in the familiar Venetian blind"—something we know today simply as vertical blinds.

A penthouse sun room had its walls and ceiling completely mirrored. The floor was green terrazzo, a modern commode had a shagreen ground-glass top, and there were murals designed and painted by Barry Faulkner.

The foyer, also designed by Victor Proetz, had painted-glass panels by Jan Juta.

As might be expected, the rooms took months to make, but in 1932 they were exhibited at the McMillen townhouse in New York. Mrs. Brown remembers Grace Fakes saying to her, "Well, they're ready; now who's going to come and look at them?" She need not have worried. During the first two weeks that the exhibition was open, more than five thousand people visited it and publicity made other cities clamor for a peek.

So at the end of 1932 the rooms and Mrs. Brown went on tour—to Boston, St. Louis, Kansas City, and Toronto—for the benefit of various unemployment relief charities (in Boston it was the Society of Architects' relief fund).

McMillen's work in miniature was not over with these model rooms. The idea caught on. While the rooms were still on display in New York, the McMillen workrooms were busy designing and making the furnishings for a series of dollhouses designed by Delano and Aldrich, a distinguished architectural firm. The idea behind these was also charitable. The com-

126

pleted houses were sold as Christmas presents, proceeds going to a fund for unemployed draftsmen.

In 1933 it was back to miniature rooms again when the American Gas Association asked Mrs. Brown to create a series for the Chicago Century of Progress Exposition, illustrating the kitchen's century of progress. The resulting rooms—kitchens of 1833, 1860, 1888, 1903, 1920, and 1933—all showed the same attention to detail lavished on the first miniature rooms.

The 1833 kitchen differed very little from its colonial forebears. It was a room where the family lived, cooked, and ate. Cooking was still done in a large kettle hanging over the fire. There was no plumbing—the water pump could be seen through the kitchen doorway—and so no sink. A dresser held pewter and pottery, and a spinning wheel stood in a corner for those

moments when the housewife found herself with nothing more immediate to do. On the mantel was a candlestick for each member of the family—all illumination was by candlelight. Tiny red peppers and onions hung from a beam and a pair of bellows stood ready at the fireplace.

By 1860, there had been great progress. Cooking was done on a coal stove which was built into the fireplace and used the chimney as a flue. Plumbing had arrived, as evidenced by the zinc sink and copper boiler. Lighting came from a gas mantle and since this kitchen was staffed and used for cooking only, there was a speaking tube to connect "upstairs" to "downstairs." Progress, however, had not yet reached floor level: white pine boards had to be scrubbed every day.

By the 1880s the gas stove had made its appearance. But it was still not reliable, so most householders

hung on to their coal stoves, which were, in any case, more economical and often the only source of heat for the room. Lighting was still by gas but plumbing had been enclosed and oilcloth made cleaning the floor much less of a chore.

The 1903 suburban kitchen showed that tile had been introduced—running as a 4-foot-high dado around the walls. Light was electric now and the gas stove, having proved itself, stood proudly—and rather ornately—on its own. The white enameled sink and draining board were other improvements that came with the turn of the century, and the first attempts to "organize" the kitchen can be spotted—a kitchen cabinet and a work table equipped with tin flour bins.

By 1920 interior decoration had reached the kitchen, though the mistress of the house had not. The alcove decorated with French provincial furniture and white ruffled curtains is the servants' dining area. Built-in cupboards have arrived and the floor is tiled.

The 1933 room displayed, naturally, the very latest in kitchen technology. And for the first time, units were placed close to each other to cut down on fetching and carrying. It was a gleaming white-and-chrome laboratory of a room, stripped to its essentials. The flooring was rubber tile, the lighting indirect. And, while a door still led to the ice room, the stove was the very last word in efficiency: insulated and with a thermostatic control!

Although Mrs. Brown says that by the time the kitchen exhibits were finished, "We all began to think we'd go cross-eyed," the model rooms served their purpose—to keep the staff busy—and more.

Not only did they benefit charity, but everywhere they appeared, they garnered publicity. As a result, by the time the country recovered from the Depression the name of McMillen was better known than ever before.

1903

Photograph by Wilbur Pippin

130

Photograph by Henry S. Fullerton 3rd

Later, Mrs. Smith used the Coromandel screens to break up the length of the living room in her new apartment.

The music room, looking through to the dining room of Mr. and Mrs. Gregory Smith's triplex apartment at 990 Fifth Avenue.

The late 1940s saw McMillen start to work for a client who was to prove unique in the firm's history. During the almost sixty years of McMillen's existence, it has not been unusual for the company to decorate several homes for the same clients, moving them from town to country and back again; following them through marriage, divorce, and remarriage and often then working for each of the two former partners; or to "inherit" the children of early clients.

But Gregory B. Smith was perhaps the ideal client. Mr. Smith is an elegant man with a gently self-deprecating sense of humor. He has naturally good taste and an interest in architecture, and McMillen's work for him, together with his relationship over the years with Natalie Davenport, the decorator in charge of all his projects, perfectly illustrates how the McMillen-client exchange works at its best.

Over the course of thirty years, McMillen and Natalie Davenport were to decorate no fewer than twelve homes for Gregory Smith.

"My wife and I had been living in the country," says Mr. Smith. "Then in 1947 my father died and we moved into his apartment at 19 East 72nd Street in New York. My mother had used McMillen; they had been recommended to her by her friend Mrs. James McDonnell.

"So I knew them and contacted them and they introduced me to Natalie Davenport—I guess Mrs. Brown allocated 'the Smith job' to Natalie. We had

This early example of the use of fabric shirred onto walls was produced by Natalie Davenport for Mrs. Smith's bedroom.

some furniture from my parents but not much. My wife quite rightly said that most of what there was was far too large for us, so we kept mostly pictures and silver.

"Then we unexpectedly produced a third child, and the arrangement of the bedrooms wasn't suitable for three children and a nurse. So we bought a four-bedroom apartment at 635 Park Avenue and Natalie worked on that with us.

"Then the Korean war came and I felt I should be doing something for my country, so I obtained a job in Washington and we moved there. We had to find a house quickly because of my job and we wanted to get the children settled into schools. I wanted to rent a house but the only one we found that was suitable was only available if we bought it. So we did and Natalie fixed it up for us.

"Two years later I left the government, but we decided to stay in Washington because we thought it better for the children. But if we were going to stay there, we felt we needed a larger house and especially one with a garden, which the first house lacked. So we found another house in Georgetown that was really quite lovely—not enormous but it had a lot of rooms.

"Natalie designed a sensational gray library for this house. It was a long narrow room with no way of widening it, but we divided it into three sitting areas and knocked out a wall on the garden side and put in a large bow window. That was my idea. We sold that house in 1957, and I'm told that that room is still the same today as it was when we sold it. Even the McMillen curtains are still there.

"We came back to New York in 1957 and bought an apartment at 990 Fifth Avenue. We were used to living in a house by this time, and didn't want to come back to a standard New York apartment. This was a triplex; large but not huge since it was on the very narrow site where the Woolworth house had been.

"The living room was also a music room where we had receptions for musicians after concerts, and Natalie had the idea of having a sofa in the dining room to make it less formal for entertaining. The library was meant to be the same as the one in Washington with gray walls again and the same furniture. There was a small upstairs sitting room with black leather furniture. My son now has some of that.

"Then my wife and I divorced, and I moved into an apartment, which I had already bought as an investment for my old age, in the Pulitzer house at 11 East 73rd Street.

"I said to Natalie that I thought it would be nice to do the apartment as though it were in Paris. It already had very high ceilings, French windows, and a fireplace, and Natalie found the *boiserie* and paneling for the living room in Paris.

"She also designed the bedroom as an octagon (actually, I think that was the idea of Albert Hadley, who was working with her on this job) and hung all the walls with fabric to set off the wonderful old Chinese bed she had found. One lady who saw it had the nerve to say she thought it 'a bit much'!

"Then in the mid-1960s, I moved to River House on East 52nd Street because I don't cook and I wanted to live in an apartment building that had restaurant facilities. Natalie did wonderful, chocolate-colored glazed walls in the living room there, with gold brocade curtains that I still have.

"About 1969 I decided to move back to the Pulitzer house apartment—I hadn't sold it—but we made a lot of changes. We made the living room less formal and turned the octagonal bedroom into a dining room so I could use the wonderful French dining-room furniture we had bought for River House. I used a small upstairs room as my bedroom. That's how the bath-

In Mr. Smith's new apartment, Mrs. Davenport also hung the bedroom walls with fabric—a pale-striped and plainly pleated silk—to create a setting for one of her great finds, a black-and-gold-lacquer Regency tester bed.

Photographs by Henry S. Fullerton 3rd

OVERLEAF: With the next move, Mr. Smith's furniture found itself set against a glamorous background of dark brown lacquered walls—a look that would soon become widely fashionable.

With its bedside push-button console, the bedroom of the 825 Fifth Avenue apartment was very much up to its minute (1974).

room, which was now off the dining room, got its sofa. It seemed strange to have a bathroom right off a dining room and I didn't need it. So I suggested we make the tub a sofa so that the room became more of a powder room and we hid the other fixtures behind a screen.

"Finally, in 1974 I bought an apartment at 825 Fifth Avenue because there was a restaurant downstairs. But my daughter married a Norwegian, and that apartment turned out to be too small when she and her family visited from Europe." Since then, Mr. Smith has continued to be peripatetic, living mostly outside New York.

During these years there were also the country houses McMillen decorated for Gregory Smith—two in Connecticut and one in France.

"The first was a funny, English-type, rather gloomy house in Connecticut," says Mr. Smith. "I remember the enclosed sun porch had a very ugly fireplace so we installed a barbecue in it and later changed all the furniture to bamboo to make it a chil-

dren's room. I had that house about five years; five years seems to be about my attention span.

"Then I bought a small château in France. We had great fun doing it. Natalie speaks fluent French and I always loved going around to the dealers in Paris with her. They thought very highly of her and I learned an awful lot about furniture from her.

"Tom Buckley worked with her on that house and the only time I ever heard of Natalie losing her temper was in the week before everything was due to be finished. There was a housekeeper who was an absolute disaster. Natalie and Tom were on their hands and knees unpacking crates and moving furniture. The housekeeper was standing watching them and Natalie suggested she help. 'Mais, madame,' said the housekeeper, 'c'est dimanche!'

"I bought that house because I've always admired French architecture and I had a dream of having a little house in France. But the children didn't like it, and it eventually seemed too far away. Still, I'd got the dream out of my system when I sold it after seven

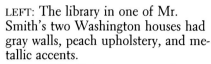

LEFT: The library in one of Mr. Smith's two Washington houses had gray walls, peach upholstery, and metallic accents.

BELOW: The living room was done in shades of ivory. The painting, an heirloom, is by Sir Henry Raeburn.

From the late 1940s until 1975, McMillen Inc. decorated twelve houses and apartments for one man: Gregory Smith. McMillen had worked for his parents, and when he inherited their New York apartment, it seemed natural for him and his wife to ask the company for help. He quickly struck up a great rapport with Natalie Davenport. From that beginning, working in close collaboration, decorator moved client to Washington and around New York's East Side and Connecticut, with one foray

to France. But it was not capricious decorating. New furniture was bought over the years, certainly, and essays were done in various styles, but most of the furniture moved with Mr. Smith and was adapted to each new surrounding, as these pictures show.

Photographs by Henry S. Fullerton 3rd

ABOVE LEFT: When the Smiths returned to New York, the Raeburn portrait was hung over a sofa in an informal dining room.

ABOVE CENTER: A study contained leather and wood pieces from the "Paris 1952" exhibition. Walls were lacquered black.

ABOVE RIGHT: The music room came complete with ceiling strapwork and wall paneling. The carved figures over the mantel are probably German.

BELOW: After their divorce, Mrs. Smith used much of the music-room furniture—Coromandel screen, chairs, chandelier, and rugs—in her new apartment.

RIGHT: In Mr. Smith's new apartment, a bathroom off the dining room became a powder room when its tub was turned into a sofa.

FAR RIGHT: He asked for a French salon, so antique French paneling was installed with a Savonnerie rug and Louis XVI furniture.

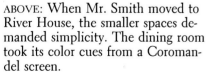

ABOVE: When Mr. Smith moved to River House, the smaller spaces demanded simplicity. The dining room took its color cues from a Coromandel screen.

RIGHT: Because of lower ceilings, the Regency bed lost its tester top in the move but the rug was retained. The walls were glazed apricot; the curtains are leather.

ABOVE: Natalie Davenport made the bedroom in this apartment octagonal and hung the walls in striped silk to show off the Regency tester bed she found for Mr. Smith. It was reputed to have been made for the Royal Pavilion at Brighton.

Photographs by Henry S. Fullerton 3rd

The last apartment Natalie Davenport decorated for Gregory Smith was completed in 1974. The background was neutral, with stippled walls and travertine floors.

LEFT: The living room took its colorings from the Ushak carpet, the library (*above*) from the kilim rug. The Directoire tub chairs in the living room and the Chinese lacquer chest used as a coffee table in the library were moved from the Connecticut house (*see next page*).

Photographs by Louis Reens

For Gregory Smith's Greek Revival house in Connecticut (*below*), only a pair of bookcases and a rug had to be bought.

RIGHT: The sofas in the library were covered with the leather from the curtains in the River House bedroom.

FAR RIGHT: The Regency bed was moved, too, and was this time set off by a small patterned chintz and a geometric carpet.

CENTER: This drawing room is one of a pair. In both, the architecture is emphasized by shades of blue.

Mr. Smith's previous Connecticut house was less formal and more colorful. Primary colors were used in the living room (*right*) and a barbecue grill was installed in the family room (*far right*).

The two rooms here were decorated for the same client at different times. Both reflect her love of tradition, but the dressing room reflects the 1940s, when the design was done, while the dining room is the result of the cleaner approach of the 1960s.

BELOW: This New England house has been in the same family for several generations. McMillen has done work here for both the present owner and his parents. The emphasis has always been on relaxed comfort and creating a background for collections, including one (*bottom*) of porcelain botanical plates in the master bedroom.

ABOVE: Real plants rival the perfection of formal depictions in the slate-floored garden room.

TOP: The present owner brought the gilt eagle from his New York apartment to guard the stairwell. His father hung the collection of bird prints.

Photographs by Michael Dunne

142

LEFT: McMillen installed bookcases, lighting, and architectural detailing in the library more than twenty years ago. As in the master bedroom (*bottom right*), the walls are glazed a soft green to show off the botanical print collection, one of the finest in private hands.

ABOVE: In a guest bedroom, more flowers appear in the design of the rug and quilts.
TOP RIGHT: Flowers are also important in the dining room; here they are printed on antique Chinese paper.

Photographs by Michael Dunne

BELOW: The needlepoint study rug was embroidered by the present owner's mother. The design incorporates scenes of the gardens.

ABOVE: The parents of the present owner used this bedroom as a sanctuary when their family was growing up. Before the eldest son inherited the house a few years ago, he and his wife lived in New York, where McMillen decorated their apartment (*top right*). When they moved, that furniture moved too, and it now blends effortlessly (*right*) with the rest of the family possessions.

Photographs by Michael Dunne and Richard Champion

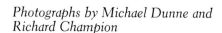

144

Photographs by Louis Reens

The last apartment of the Smith-Davenport partnership was this pared-down design done in the mid-1970s.

years. A Frenchman bought it, and I heard that the first thing he was going to do was to eliminate the beautiful black-white-and-brown bathroom. It was too sensational for him.

"So I then bought another house in Connecticut. It was Greek Revival, and I sometimes wonder if it wasn't the prettiest house of them all. All the architecture was there, but Natalie very cleverly picked it out in blues. This was at the time of my second move to the Pulitzer house and the Chinese bed had lost its bedroom. So we moved it here along with other furnishings from River House and France."

One of the fascinating things about all these moves is the way furnishings moved from one place to another, very often finding a place in different rooms in different houses. The buildup over the years had been gradual, but by the time this house came to be furnished and even though Mr. Smith also had his New York apartment, only two major pieces—a pair of Empire bookcases for the library—and a rug had to be bought.

Of course, things changed but not in a profligate way. When furnishings could not find a place in a new environment they were either sold—the Chinese bed to a decorator, a Coromandel screen to William Paley—or given away. The Art Deco chairs from the library in Washington went first to Mr. Smith's New York office and then were donated to a school. Other rugs and furniture were given to children or godchildren.

"People wonder about me and all my moves," Gregory Smith admits. "Part of the story is that I majored in architecture at Yale but I was a terrible draftsman and I just couldn't go on with it.

"But it still interested me. It was a challenge and I enjoyed it. It was sort of a private career for me, although as I look back, during the years I was married we always thought we had a good reason for moving. First, needing another bedroom for the children; then moving to Washington and needing a house quickly; then deciding to stay there and wanting a bigger house with a garden of some kind; and finally, deciding to

When Gregory Smith bought his
dream house in France (*above*),
Natalie Davenport designed a stylish
black leather buttoned and fringed
bed (*opposite page*) but shopped in
Paris for the more traditional dining
room (*right*).

move back to New York. It always seemed quite
logical.

"So, although I enjoyed doing it, it wasn't as capricious as some people might think. And I got on
very well with Natalie. She's very reserved, but I am
very fond of her and I think I was one of her favorite
clients.

"We always discussed concepts and then she'd
come up with two or three schemes and we'd either
pick one or compromise. She never tried to force her
choice on us and I think she liked the fact that both
Mrs. Smith and I knew what we liked. She often said
to me that the worst clients were the ones who
couldn't make up their minds or didn't know what
they liked.

"It's incredible when you think about it, but I
never had a fight with Natalie. Looking back, there
was a hall at 635 Park Avenue and a blue bedroom at
990 Fifth that I didn't like. I remember thinking when
she showed us the paper for that room—it was blue
and crinkly—that it didn't look really like my wife or
me, but it's very hard to like everything you've
picked."

Photographs by Ernest Silva

At the same time, the furniture collected over nearly thirty years was used to furnish Mr. Smith's country house in Connecticut, shown on this page and the next page. Other views of this design odyssey appear in color on pages 137–40.

How does Natalie Davenport remember the Smiths?

"They were virtually my first clients when I came back to McMillen after the war. Mrs. Brown gave them to me—one decorator was always appointed to be in charge of each job.

"I remember they had all this superlative English furniture they'd inherited and that I couldn't stand it. It was all the dreary *bois des roses* look and I went as far as I felt I could and pepped it up a little bit. Then, after a year or two, they moved again and I pepped that job up even more.

"Little by little I was modernizing their things and then, of course, they moved to Washington. I was always using things we already had but there were new things to find too and it got more interesting with each job. By then I was starting to know their tastes extremely well, so it was easier for me. I liked them and we became good friends—we'd have lunch and so forth.

"Then they moved back to New York to 990 Fifth Avenue, and we did fascinating things there.

Gregory Smith was always very musical, and you always had to take that interest into account when you were decorating the main room. I found some curious gilt animals, each playing different instruments, that I put over the mantel in the main room here. No one knows where they're from but I think perhaps they originally were part of a German console organ. Anyway, the people who bought that apartment from the Smiths insisted on those figures being included in the sale.

"That room also had English oak paneling that most people, at the time, would have painted or ripped out. But we kept it. I remember the first marbleized wallpapers had just come out and a new kind of stucco paper with gold in it and we used those for the halls.

"Then after they got divorced, I did apartments for both of them. Gregory bought a house in Connecticut that I adored because I got some Early American furniture—my great passion—into it.

"Then came the Pulitzer house, which he wanted to look like a Paris apartment. Grace Fakes and I struggled for months over the designs for *boiserie* and paneling and then I went to Paris and found the perfect paneling there. The ceilings were enormously high in that living room and we had to lower them to fit the paneling.

"That's also when I found the Chinese bed in New York. I was so excited about that I could hardly stand it. You see, I really loved work, and I'd get so excited about it and I think that communicated itself to the Smiths. Maybe they spent more money than they intended to—I don't know, we never went through a budget together—but I'd get so excited and it was never a question of, Will I make a lot of money? It was just what was beautiful. Not very good business sense, but a lot of fun.

"Then came the house in France and that was the hardest one of all, although in a way it was also the most fun once the worst was over. But we'd go there (Tom Buckley was working with me) and we'd work so hard we wouldn't bother to stop for lunch—or if we did, it would be radishes and cheese or something from the local market. I remember that where I would have just dumped it out on a table and eaten, Tom always arranged it on trays elegantly so it looked like a real lunch.

"Back in New York, Mr. Smith moved from the Pulitzer house to River House, and I did what I think was the first-ever brown-lacquered room. Actually, Billy Baldwin had done a red-lacquered room, which is maybe where I got the idea from, but I had to do something to cut the glare. That room faced the East River, which reflected sunlight back into it. I was told

later that 'Sister' Parish thought it awful! The Chinese bed went to River House but without its canopy because the ceiling wasn't high enough.

"Then it was back to the Pulitzer house, where we made the master bedroom into the dining room and the guest room Mr. Smith's bedroom. For that, all we needed to find was a rug. We had everything else.

"About the same time, Mr. Smith bought a Greek Revival house in Stonington, Connecticut. There, we wanted the house to be extremely livable, the way a country house should be. The blue walls in the drawing room took a good deal of discussion, but I think the two shadings emphasize the strong architectural element of the room.

"The last apartment I did was really a *pied-à-terre* and very modern but still with a lot of things from previous homes.

"It really was fun moving things from place to place for the same client. I was terribly lucky the way I was constantly working for Gregory Smith. As far as I'm concerned, I had nice angels watching over me."

1940

A year later, the same bust as that shown in the picture opposite was displayed differently.

Photograph by Hans van Nes

A Neo-classical corner of the McMillen townhouse in 1940.

Photograph by Emelie Danielson

Before the 1939 New York World's Fair was over, Europe was at war, and whatever direct influence European design might have had on America was postponed for the duration.

In the following two years, before the United States joined the conflict, the American design community remained relatively unaffected and, indeed, began to pay attention to the innovations of its own designers such as Eero Saarinen (the son of Eliel) and Charles Eames, both of whom, though believing in functionalism, searched for a softer expression of its austerity.

Their experimental work, shown in a 1940 exhibition, "Organic Design in Home Furnishing," at New York's Museum of Modern Art, was to have a lasting influence on the world of American interior design, as was the continuing work of Walter Gropius and Mies van der Rohe who, like many of their countrymen, had fled Germany to find sanctuary in the United States.

In another room of the townhouse, a
pair of Directoire chairs flanked a
small commode, while two eighteenth-century mirrors reflected each
other.

"Organic" design stressed flexibility in both materials and function. Laminated woods were used with metal, seating was designed to accommodate the curves of the human body, and storage components were designed to offer a variety of arrangements.

By the time World War II ended, the world was unalterably changed and these changes, as always, were reflected in the design world. Both socially and economically, the changes were immense.

Socially, men who had fought for freedom demanded an improved standard of living as a reward for their sacrifices, and women, who had taken men's places on factory floors throughout the country, had made themselves a permanent force to be reckoned with in the American job market.

Economically, the world seemed exhausted and the immediate postwar years were ones of austerity. But industry, especially in the United States, quickly picked itself up and, helped by a growing national sense of optimism as well as some significant industrial and scientific advances, achieved in part through the pressures of war, rapidly went into overdrive.

America boomed, and by the end of the 1940s she was the worldwide symbol of material progress. Never had so many made so much so quickly.

Industrial innovations originally designed for military use were quickly adapted to peacetime needs. Whole new categories of materials sprang up—metal alloys, synthetic fibers, and the world of plastics that we now almost take for granted.

Alloys, with either aluminum or magnesium as their basic metals, changed furniture design because they offered a combination of great lightness and great strength.

Synthetic fibers included the now ubiquitous polyester and other fabrics whose great advantage was that they cleaned more easily and in some cases were more hard-wearing than natural fibers.

But it was the advent of plastics that most changed the shape of design—especially where seating was concerned. Injection-molded plastic could be designed as sculpture; the molten plastic was poured into a mold where it hardened into strong finished pieces that melded grace and comfort.

American designers quickly adopted these new materials along with molded plywood (which both Charles Eames and Eero Saarinen had used before the war but which aviation technology had since improved) to give America a preeminence in the world of design that it had never before achieved.

Indeed, two of the most famous chairs in the world were designed during the last years of war. In 1945 Charles Eames designed a side chair of steel tubing and molded plywood that is seen today in offices

This mirror, bought in 1935 by Eleanor Brown, is similar to one donated by her for the restoration of Blair House.

Photographs by Hans van Nes

Photograph by Emelie Danielson

In the early years, the McMillen showrooms were decorated to resemble the private house the rooms once composed. Here and on the next two pages, the drawing room, a bedroom, and the dining room are shown as they looked in the early 1930s.

Photograph by Carl Klein Studios

Photograph by Drix Duryea

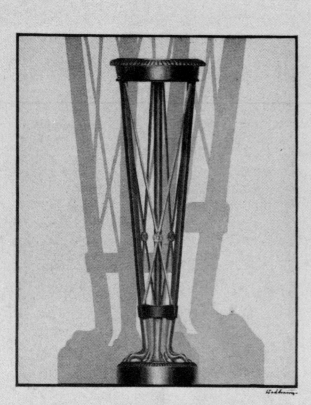
and schools throughout the world, and in 1946 Eero Saarinen designed a molded plastic shell, upholstered in foam rubber and supported by a tubular steel frame, that was immediately called the "womb chair."

Designers were also aware of changes going on within the home as the country recovered from the war and started looking to the future. New was "in"—but it was also necessary.

The enormous new middle class that sprang up in the late 1940s could afford homes, cars, refrigerators. A building boom was on. Mass production had never been so important or so possible. It was the start of suburbia.

Postwar houses for the middle class were smaller than their prewar counterparts, so interior space had to be used more creatively and efficiently. In addition, working wives did not want to spend their evenings doing housework, so the emphasis was on materials and furnishings that did not have dirt-catching nooks and crannies, on fabrics that were easy to clean, and on labor-saving devices.

At the same time, even the rich had to readjust their way of living. The war had brought about the almost total departure of the servant class. Men who had fought in Europe or the Pacific and women who had supported the war effort in well-paid factory jobs were not prepared to go back to being butlers and maids. And now the new immigrants (traditionally a source of household help) had higher ambitions.

So, in the homes of the rich, living might still be gracious but some rooms, especially kitchens, changed. It was in the kitchen, which now emphasized efficiency and low labor costs, that the effects both of the availability of new industrial materials and of electronic breakthroughs and improved factory methods were most clearly to be seen.

Kitchen design was also important in middle-class homes, where working wives wanted to live and entertain informally. And for them, other rooms were redesigned as well.

A conventional house suffered when it was built to only three-quarters of the size of its prewar sister. The conventional divisions into living room, dining room, and bedrooms produced a series of small, cramped rooms. So the new rooms were designed to be dual-purpose. The ranch-style house was born, designed with one open space that was used for living, dining, and entertaining and, very often, with only a partition dividing it from the kitchen.

Furniture was used to partition space, either visually, by using seating groups to define areas, or physically, using storage units as room dividers.

The move to a more informal life-style had its roots in more than economic necessity. A way of living

This unprepossessing former school-house became McMillen's showroom in Houston in 1940.

popular in California had started to make its influence felt throughout the country. That life-style—open and outdoors and later to be dubbed "laid-back"—seemed to suit the mood of the country as a whole as it geared up in the late 1940s for a new decade which was to prove to be a time of almost unlimited—and previously undreamed-of—material growth.

With McMillen solidly successful and the United States not yet at war, Eleanor Brown started the 1940s with a brand-new venture. Never one to rest on her laurels, she decided, with some prescience, to open the first branch of McMillen Inc. in Houston, Texas.

"We were doing a lot of work down there," Ethel Smith recalls, "and there certainly was a lot of money." Eleanor Brown may also have wanted to raise the taste level of Texans. A good friend, the architect John Staub, was designing and building the most elegant houses in Texas, but their furnishings did not always live up to the standards of his architecture. Ethel Smith remembers there was a great deal of resistance in that state to "fashionable New York decorators. In those days, Texans wanted to be Texans, and it was very difficult to sell them a real antique. They loved modern reproductions."

Inside the Houston building, however, it would have been difficult to
imagine anything less like a school-
house.

The Houston showrooms were also used as a gallery for art exhibitions. These shows included one of horses (*this page*) and sporting prints in aid of the British War Relief Society, one of French Impressionist paintings (*opposite page, top*), and one of the works of the sculptor Boris Lovet-Lorski.

Photograph by George Hampton Matchett

164

So in February 1940 Eleanor Brown presided over the opening of the new showroom at 2503 West-heimer Road in the even then fashionable River Oaks section of Houston.

The white-painted brick building had been a schoolhouse and then a civic center. It was a plain building, and Mrs. Brown regarded it as much an art gallery as a decorating showroom.

Always interested in promoting the arts, she arranged exhibitions with the help of such New York galleries as Wildenstein and Knoedler. In the first two years these ranged from the work of French Impressionists to Texan artists. As the effects of war started to be felt, exhibitions were mounted for charities. There was an exhibition of British sporting prints and sculpture in aid of the British War Widows' Relief Fund and an exhibition of the work of "foreign artists now in this country and consequently available for portrait commissions," as it was delicately put.

But fine furniture was not forgotten, and as in New York, it was always presented as a complete room setting. Inside the plain brick schoolhouse could be found a Directoire room one month, a Louis XVI room the next.

But the war forced Mrs. Brown to close down the Houston outpost in 1943, when it had become impossible to ship things. And though during the brief three years of its existence it had been successful, Mrs. Brown was never tempted to reopen it.

"There was so much going on after the war and attitudes changed. It was just too much trouble to reopen, and even though we do more work now in Houston than ever before, I think one of the reasons for that is that Houstonians now like to have a *New York* decorator. That may sound snobby, but they do like that and they like to come to New York. Also, there's so little good workmanship around now, and most of it is in New York. We have to have most things made in New York and shipped, whether it's to Texas or Florida."

America's entry into the Second World War also meant that McMillen lost most of its good workmen to active service or to jobs directly related to the war effort. True, there was little work to be done during those years, but the loss of the carefully trained and nurtured staff was a hard blow.

Without the staff to make miniature rooms— even if they had wanted to—and with virtually no work, Eleanor Brown decided to concentrate on exhibitions. Most of the Houston exhibitions had their premieres in New York, but in addition there were others that did not travel.

Among the most important of these was the African art show McMillen mounted in early 1942. This

McMillen decorated this indoor swimming pool and adjoining bar area (*opposite page*) in the 1940s for Doris Duke.

was one of the very first exhibitions in America to be devoted to Negro art—a combination of old and primitive African sculpture and paintings by modern black artists.

As she did during the Depression, Mrs. Brown also kept McMillen's name in the public eye by designing room settings for manufacturers, retailers, and magazines. All promoted products of various kinds—fabrics, china, wallcoverings, and crystal—but at the same time all promoted McMillen.

Therefore, as at the end of the Depression, at the end of the Second World War the name of McMillen was as widely known as ever. Mrs. Brown calmly regrouped her forces, and the company found itself in as much demand as it had been five years earlier.

McMillen also found itself with more competition than ever before. The established few were still there: Elsie de Wolfe, Rose Cumming, and Ruby Ross Wood, whose careers predated Mrs. Brown's; Syrie Maugham, Dorothy Draper, and "Sister" Parish, who had carved out their careers in the 1930s. But just as the immediate postwar years saw America take the world lead in developing new materials and new design concepts, so they also saw a whole new crop of American decorators spring up.

For the first time, the most important of these were men: William Pahlmann, who made his name designing room settings for Lord & Taylor, and who designed modern furniture for traditional interiors; George Stacey, who blended period furniture against clean backgrounds in high style; Edward Wormley, who designed practical furniture for various companies, including Drexel and Dunbar; T. H. Robsjohn-Gibbings, who promoted simplicity and modern American design; and Billy Baldwin, who pioneered dark, shiny-lacquered walls and the use of fresh cotton print fabrics.

Eleanor Brown had lost the friendship and advice of William Odom with his death in 1942, but he was succeeded as president of the Parsons School of Design (of which Mrs. Brown was now a trustee) by another close friend, Van Day Truex.

In a 1980 article in *House & Garden* Billy Baldwin remembered those days: "We were the upstarts and between our younger ideas and the fabulous and growing array of fabrics, papers and colors everywhere, decorating in America was just about as emotional an art as it had ever been.

"As decorators became more and more creative, art—as itself, not as ornament—and sculpture which had been almost universally rejected before, began to appear in contemporary rooms. And in a grand departure from the European antiques and FFF (Fine French Furniture) now coveted and collected by everyone who could afford them, people began to notice that America had produced some quite wonderful furniture too."

Running parallel to these experiments with the new was, as the 1940s ended, a revival in traditionalism and eclecticism. This "bring back romance" movement was a natural reaction against the hardships of the war years, but it borrowed from more cultures—Greek and Oriental in addition to English, French, and Italian—than had any design movement in the past.

At McMillen, clients still sought FFF, and the firm obliged them. But Eleanor Brown, always curious about the new, embraced the fresh ideas as well—especially the new prominence of modern art and the accompanying growth of interest in crafts and craftsmen.

ABOVE AND OPPOSITE PAGE: A few choice pieces of Oriental art are the only decoration in this private library. McMillen wisely made no attempt to scale the seating up to the room's massive proportions.

OVERLEAF: In this 1940 living room, an antique Aubusson rug and silk damask curtains and upholstery provided low-keyed pattern and texture.

Photograph by André Kertész

In the same house, an architecturally ordinary bedroom came to life with painted furniture, a wallpaper-and-*faux-marbre* screen, and a flamboyant Venetian mirror.

Photograph by André Kertész

1950

By the start of the 1950s, the whole Western world was taking its cue from the United States. Whatever was new and exciting emanated from this country, and Americans realized it.

The millions of new members of the middle class were becoming more affluent by the year, and having money to spend on luxuries rather than necessities for the first time, they became design-conscious.

The architect reigned supreme now that houses were designed as machines for living. Machines themselves became part of every home and labor-saving devices proliferated as Americans began their long and continuing love affair with gadgets.

Electronic advances affected the house in less obvious ways too. Large windows that in previous years would have turned rooms into hothouses in summer no longer had to be avoided, thanks to air conditioning, which had become cheap and easily available.

This pearwood folding desk was designed by Maxime Old. The writing surface was covered in green leather, the pigeonholes in red leather.

The metal frames of this sofabed and chair were covered in tan saddle-stitched leather.

New vistas opened up for architects, now that windows could be as big as desired. Almost every architect worth his salt designed a house with walls of glass—the most famous being Philip Johnson's own Connecticut house—that happily defied stones. The expanses of glass and steel and concrete demanded that furnishings follow their simplicity and sleekness, and irrevocably changed interior design.

Another irrevocable change was the introduction of the television set. A house was not a home without one, but its obtrusive presence created a design problem that has not yet been completely solved. It immediately became a focal point of any room it was in, especially since many new houses lacked fireplaces. In the 1950s (and indeed until the 1970s) the one-eyed monster was most commonly disguised as a "beautiful piece of furniture," but there was something a little vacant about furniture arrangements that focused on a blank credenza. However, this was but a minor flaw in a design world that had entered one of its most exciting decades.

The prosperity of the middle class allowed it to indulge its materialistic dreams, and in so doing its members started to explore design and designers for the first time. They were receptive to new ideas—conservatism in this respect was at a low ebb—and America had the architects and designers ready to oblige.

What resulted was the Contemporary Style, a design vernacular stemming mostly from American and Scandinavian sources that was created partly to satisfy the needs of the new clean, spare, and informal architecture but was also a response to the public's new interest in design in the home.

Scandinavian design—called Swedish Modern—had enormous worldwide impact in the 1950s. Its prewar genesis had already been seen in America when the work of Alvar Aalto was shown at the 1939 World's Fair in New York.

In the 1950s designers such as Aalto in Finland and Arne Jacobsen in Denmark worked within the same design ethic as the International Modernists but still used that most traditional of materials, wood. The emphasis was on craft, and the beauty of the wood was left to speak for itself. That, perhaps, was the reason for the great success of Swedish Modern. Scandinavian furniture adopted the new shapes of the machine-made materials but provided them, handcrafted and sculpted, in a more expected material. The new consumer society in America saw more of the luxury it desired in wood than in steel.

This newfound consumerism also affected American design. Here too, materials became more luxurious—leather was used a lot—and there was a certain

Gilbert Poillerat designed this dining
table and console. Both are of marble
on gilded wrought-iron bases.

desire among the public for a sleek, sophisticated look
to go with their new sleek, sophisticated lives. International Modernism regained its popularity but in a less
stark expression than formerly.

Both these elements amalgamated during the
early 1950s to produce what came to be known as the
Contemporary Style. At its best, the Contemporary
Style had a certain restrained elegance; at its worst, a
cold self-consciousness.

But although this style evolved to some degree
from the pure creativity of designers excited about the
possibilities of the new materials, it owed its development much more to the overriding architectural problem of how to make the most of limited space. Some
pieces of furniture—armoires, bureaus, chests, and
desks—virtually disappeared. For, in an architectural
vernacular that built in closets, cabinets, and multipurpose wall units, they were no longer necessary. And as
ceilings became lower, overhead lighting lost popular-

ity for there was not the height to hang even a modest
chandelier.

Another architectural influence—walls made
largely of glass, which broke down the division
between indoors and outdoors—promoted the move
toward informal living that was also becoming an economic and social necessity.

Therefore, what furniture was necessary for this
streamlined architecture (mostly seating and tables)
also had to have clean, simple lines. And because so
little furniture was used in comparison with previous
styles, each piece took on its own importance in the
overall scheme of things. It was this importance that
fueled the interest and new design consciousness of
what had become by the end of the decade a vast
consumer-oriented public.

The only problem was that these masterpieces of
modern design—Charles Eames's leather-and-molded-
plywood lounge chair and ottoman, Mies van der

Rohe's leather-and-steel "Barcelona" chair, Eero Saarinen's molded-plastic and foam-rubber "womb" and "tulip" chairs, and Arne Jacobsen's reinforced-plastic-and-foam-rubber "egg" and "swan" chairs, to name but a few—were still expensive.

It would not be until the 1960s that production would become sufficiently mechanized to bring costs down to the level of the average budget. In the meantime, these designs remained within the preserve of the rich and their decorators.

In February 1950 Eleanor Brown celebrated her sixtieth birthday. She had thought about retiring, but when the time came to make a decision, she found it impossible to withdraw from all the excitement and change she saw around her.

"There was suddenly a wide growth of extraordinary discernment and taste," she says. "For the first time in almost two hundred years, people could associate a fine piece of furniture, a plate, or a rug with the artist who designed it. Modern designers, as in the age of Chippendale, Robert Adam, and later Duncan Phyfe, sought new motifs in ancient sources and interpreted them in the materials of the day.

"At McMillen we still believed, as we have always done, in the use of natural materials, but if the new man-made materials seemed right, we used them."

Although the bulk of McMillen's clients had always been top-drawer, the 1950s were the decade that saw the firm really consolidate its reputation as decorator to the socially registered. Its staff's expertise in a wide variety of styles and periods; its ability to handle jobs of any size anywhere down to the last detail; its reputation for honesty, built up now over twenty-five years; its conviction that a room must fit the client rather than reflect McMillen (although all their work bears the firm's indefinable stamp)—all these combined to attract new clients. The names speak for themselves: Mr. and Mrs. Henry Ford II, Mrs. Marjorie Merriweather Post, Millicent Rogers, Mr. and Mrs. C. Douglas Dillon.

To cope with the increased work load, Mrs. Brown expanded McMillen again. In 1951 Betty Sherrill joined the firm fresh from Parsons.

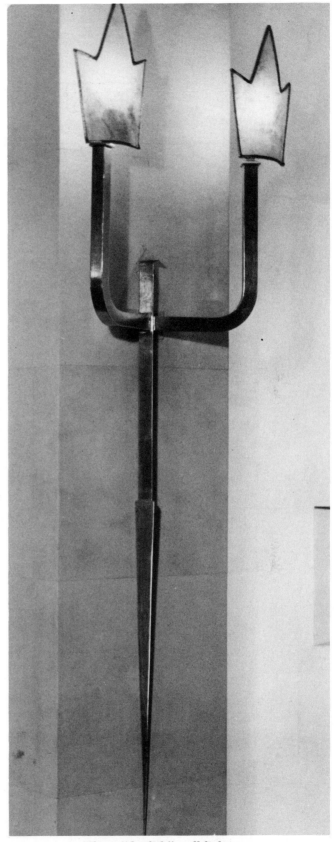

More of Poillerat's wrought-iron designs: a pair of marble-topped guéridons and a dining table with a green-lacquered top. The screen is also lacquer.

These "devilish" wall lights were made of gold leaf on wood.

181

Photographs by Henry S. Fullerton 3rd

Two ways of using panels: boldly patterned fabric used in a bedroom (*previous page*) and classic ivory-painted wood with an arched mirror.

Irene Walker joined soon after Betty Sherrill, and by the mid-1950s Albert Hadley (who had been turned down for a job in 1947 by Mrs. Brown but had taken her advice and gone to Parsons) had finally found a place with the firm.

By the end of the 1950s Grace Fakes, her eyesight failing, was talking about retiring and so, to strengthen the design department which she had headed since 1926, Tom Buckley and then, early in 1960, John Drews (both again straight from Parsons) came to McMillen.

The range of work done by McMillen during the 1950s was enormous and illustrates the wide variety of options that became available to designers during that decade. There was a villa in Jamaica for William and "Babe" Paley, several apartments and houses in several states and styles for Gregory B. Smith, a dramatic bachelor apartment for Raymond Guest, and grandscale New York apartments for Ambassador and Mrs. Angier Biddle Duke, Mrs. Diego Suarez (the former Mrs. Marshall Field), the second Mrs. Field, and Abby Rockefeller Mauzé, among others.

A rich brown-lacquered screen with a modernistic Oriental design was a feature of the "Paris 1952" exhibition.

Photograph by Henry S. Fullerton 3rd

As Europe recovered from the Second World War, Eleanor Brown resumed her regular trips to Europe and found herself increasingly impressed by the work being done in France by young artists and artisans. In 1952 she presented the first exhibition of postwar European furniture design shown in the United States— the whole McMillen townhouse was redecorated to give this new furniture its best setting. Partly because of her espousal of young French craftsmen, the French government later that year appointed Mrs. Brown a Chevalier of the Legion of Honor.

ABOVE: A bachelor apartment featured leather furniture. Tan saddle-stitched desk drawers resembled briefcases.

RIGHT: In a family dining room, the table was of green lacquer and wrought iron; the chairs were covered in quilted satin.

Photographs by Henry S. Fullerton 3rd

RIGHT: A bookcase was made of chrome "ladders," covered in black leather with elm shelves slung between them.

LEFT: More black leather in the bachelor dining area. The coach lamp was suspended from the wall by leather straps.

Photographs by Henry S. Fullerton 3rd

BELOW: The living room of Mr. and Mrs. Alfred Gwynne Vanderbilt takes its tone from the Bessarabian rug. The leather-covered chairs are Louis XVI.

RIGHT: A mirrored panel in a hallway is a McMillen hallmark. The glass in this mirror is smoked, and the drawings are by Van Day Truex.

ABOVE: The bedroom is kept simple, in shades of off-white and rose.

RIGHT: For the library, Grace Fakes designed the mantel to incorporate hand-painted porcelain plaques.

Photographs by Henry S. Fullerton 3rd

This Long Island house was decorated by McMillen more than twenty years ago and remains virtually unchanged, as these pictures, taken last year, show. Although the house is well lived-in, the furnishings show little sign of wear and tear.

LEFT: The dark green gun room is appropriately masculine.

BOTTOM LEFT: The Adam-style mantel in the living room is flanked by a pair of Queen Anne mirrors, while the curtains were hand-embroidered in Paris. The upholstery is of yellow damask. One chair—the owner's favorite—showed enough wear to require reupholstering last year.

BELOW: The entrance hall has a classic, McMillen-designed marble floor as well as a wrought-iron and green-lacquer table.

ABOVE: Comfort is stressed in the library, with its Coromandel screen and antique Savonnerie rug. The tub chair has since been recaned.

Photographs by Michael Dunne

Betty Sherrill, president of McMillen Inc. since 1976, has been with the firm almost thirty years. Her two houses—one summer, one winter—and her New York apartment reflect the diversity of her taste, which ranges from the frankly traditional to country casual to low-maintenance simplicity.

BELOW: Black is used as a cooling accent in the master bedroom of the winter house. The chests and chairs are black lacquer inlaid with mother of pearl, while the chaise is new wicker painted black.

ABOVE: Easy-care ceramic floor tiles run throughout the public rooms and out onto the terraces.

ABOVE RIGHT: The living room is kept neutral with natural wicker, beige linen, rattan screens. Small flashes of color come from cushions, flowers, and the Robert Natkin painting.

RIGHT: Antique pieces—Thai statues, a Chinese lacquered chest, and an Italian console—stand out in high relief against the pristine architecture of the entrance hall.

Photographs by Michael Dunne

LEFT: A mirrored window wall gives additional depth to the traditionally furnished New York living room. But good-looking tradition need not be expensive: the curtain fabric cost one dollar per yard in 1968.

BELOW LEFT: In contrast to the pastel-toned living room, the library/dining room was made dramatic with walls glazed a deep watermelon and seating covered in either dark brown leather or a zebra-print linen.

For the summer house, a *trompe l'oeil* striped awning brought whimsy into the poolside cabana.

Photograph by Tom Leonard

OVERLEAF: Always aware of even occasional contrasts, McMillen made
sure that a bedroom with a calm
scheme led from this richly decorated
hall.

HERE AND ON THE NEXT FOUR PAGES: As is not unusual for the firm, McMillen decorated these rooms in several houses between the 1930s and the 1950s for one client. All rooms were firmly rooted in tradition, but as they have done for many clients over the years, McMillen rang subtle changes with their designs for *boiserie*, cornices, and pilasters.

A library (*above and opposite page*) had bleached wood paneling, a Chinese rug, and an unusual oval desk.

Photographs by Emelie Danielson

Eighteenth-century English furniture
in a dining room (*below*) included a
rare bow-front sideboard.

A twelve-fold Coromandel screen was
divided in half, with sections placed
at either side of a living room above.

Photographs by Emelie Danielson

196

Another living-room view. The secretary is red lacquer and of the Queen Anne period. Other furniture is English.

The use of *boiserie* provided a completely different setting for the dining room of the client's country house on Long Island (*above*).

A color scheme of off-white, yellow, beige, and light brown for another living room (*right*) was drawn from the soft shades in the Louis XVI Aubusson rug. (Rendering by Elizabeth Hoopes)

Photographs by Hans van Nes

The imposing proportions of the drawing room at left were achieved by taking two apartments, one above the other, and removing the upper floor. The upper tier of windows was blocked out, and the curtains were draped high on the walls to give an illusion of height to the remaining openings.

Strong architectural details were used in this library (*above*), as well as in one on page 194; in both the shelves were edged with gold-embossed scalloped leather.

199

But three undertakings—each of them different and each in a different part of the country—stand out. One was the restoration of Rosedown, a 150-year-old plantation house in St. Francisville, Louisiana; the second was the creation of an eighteenth-century French interior for the Georgian-style mansion of Mr. and Mrs. Henry Ford II in Grosse Pointe, Michigan; and the third was an important exhibition in McMillen's New York townhouse that gave America its first look at postwar French design and was partly responsible for the French government deciding to make Eleanor Brown a Chevalier of the Legion of Honor in 1952.

The commission to restore Rosedown came to McMillen by chance.

"I was at a bankers' convention with my husband," Betty Sherrill says, "and fell into conversation with another of the wives. Her name was Mrs. Milton Underwood, and she told me how she had bought an old plantation almost by accident.

"She lived in Houston but had been in Natchez with her garden club when someone asked the group if any of them would like to buy a plantation. She had gone to look at it, and that evening, when her husband asked her how she had spent her day, she said, 'I nearly bought a plantation.' 'Why didn't you?' he asked. 'I think I will,' she said and that's exactly what she did the next day!

"The house was almost beyond repair, and the Underwoods were building a new house to live in on the grounds. After that meeting at the convention, she asked McMillen to work on their new house and that's how we started off.

"But Mr. Underwood became more and more interested in restoring the land, which was also in a terrible state, and from that they both became interested in restoring the old house and they asked us to help."

Since neither Mr. nor Mrs. Underwood wanted to live in the house, they decided to restore it to what it would have been like when first lived in in 1835, when it was built by Daniel Turnbull, a wealthy young planter, for his bride, and then to open it to the public.

For McMillen it was a great challenge. Not only did that decision mean Victoriana—a style in which the firm had rarely worked—but saving the fabric of the house was a problem.

"It was a mess," Ethel Smith, who along with Betty Sherrill was in charge of the team that worked on Rosedown, remembers with a shudder. "There were snakes, holes in the floor, cobwebs and filth. Wallpaper was stained and peeling; furniture and windows were broken. It was a nightmare."

The decay had been insidious. The two elderly sisters who had owned the house, descendants of the Turnbulls, had eked out a living over the years by gradually selling most of the furniture that could easily be moved, and the twenty-three acres of once immaculate gardens and cotton fields were completely overgrown.

When Rosedown was built, the South was at its height as a center of wealth and fashion. Rich young planters like Turnbull vied with each other in building bigger and better mansions, most of which, like Rosedown, were basically Georgian in style with Greek Revival touches.

Like their peers, Daniel Turnbull and his wife, Martha, took pride in furnishing their house with the latest and finest furniture from Europe as well as having local craftsmen make pieces especially for them. Rosedown, when the Turnbulls moved in, epitomized the affluence of the pre–Civil War South.

Most of these glories had gone when McMillen began work and those that remained—mainly large pieces of furniture that could not easily have been sold or moved—were broken or rotting.

"But we saved every piece of furniture that could be saved," Ethel Smith says. "We put up a quonset hut on the grounds and moved everything out to it. We hired local workmen to restore as much as they could, and for a year that was one of the best workshops anywhere. In the meantime, there was an absolute army of builders, plasterers, and carpenters at work on the house itself."

The long-dead Mrs. Turnbull also turned out to be a great help. She had kept all the original bills of sale and made meticulous inventories as the house was built and furnished. Luckily, these still existed, and using them as a guide, Ethel Smith, with the help of Albert Hadley, plunged into research.

No attempt was made to find the original furnishings. McMillen and Mr. and Mrs. Underwood decided to furnish Rosedown as the Turnbulls—who had obviously been a well-traveled and sophisticated couple—would have done.

"We'd find things and say to ourselves, 'Now, if I was Daniel Turnbull, would I have bought it?'" Albert Hadley recalls. "The inventories gave clues and we had a good idea of their taste from the things that were still there and that's how we worked. There's a swan cradle we found in New York that's now in one of the bedrooms and I *know* the Turnbulls would have bought it if they'd seen it."

Also as the Turnbulls had done, McMillen bought furniture in various styles from various countries. The set of painted chairs in the breakfast room had originally been made for England's Brighton Pavilion. The dining-room chairs are American, probably by Duncan Phyfe.

In 1954 McMillen was one of several design firms that took "Paris in New York" as their theme for a series of room settings. After the success of their exhibition of modern French furniture two years previously, McMillen chose to return to the traditional. Grace Fakes turned a soldier's nineteenth-century iron-and-brass campaign bed into a feminine bower by hanging dotted-swiss muslin from a gilded coronet that was supported by a thin metal frame. Mirror paneling on the window wall gave an illusion of spaciousness. The windows were also hung in white net, repeating the design of the bed hangings.

The commission to decorate the home of Anne and Henry Ford II in Grosse Pointe, Michigan, was one of McMillen's greatest coups in the 1950s. The furnishings were to be in part English but mostly French, all eighteenth-century and the finest money could buy. The ensuing "treasure hunt" around Europe and among the top American antique dealers undertaken by Anne Ford and Marion Morgan, McMillen's expert on eighteenth-century French and English design, resulted in one of the finest interiors ever put together from scratch. It would be almost impossi-

ble for anyone—no matter how wealthy—to put together a collection of such a richness and quality today.

ABOVE: In the entrance hall, a round ottoman was centered on an Adam rug. The mantel and chairs are also Adam. The painting over the mantel is a Manet; the sculpture is by Rodin.

LEFT: In Mr. Ford's study, a rare kidney-shaped walnut William and Mary desk.

Photographs by Henry S. Fullerton 3rd

LEFT: The entrance to the stair-hall was flanked on one side by an English biscuitware glass-domed clock on a satinwood-and-marquetry pedestal almost certainly made by Chippendale.

TOP RIGHT: The ladies' powder room also had an antique *parquet de Versailles* floor. The dressing table is flanked by a pair of Louis XV screens.

ABOVE: The dining-room walls were covered in white-and-gold damask. The Adam chairs are part of an extremely rare set of twenty-four.

LEFT: In a guest room, twin canopy beds were hung in silk taffeta. Even the canopy linings were elegantly trimmed.

Photographs by Henry S. Fullerton 3rd

RIGHT: Grinling Gibbons paneling found in England was used on the library walls. The red lacquer secretary is Queen Anne; the painting is by Degas.

BELOW: The breakfast room was paneled with antique Chinese wallpaper. Niches displayed Mrs. Ford's collections of porcelain. The green lacquer table is contemporary.

ABOVE: For Mrs. Ford's bedroom, blue silk was stretched on the walls and the white satin bedspread and bed hangings were hand-embroidered in Paris following the design of an old document print.

RIGHT: The living-room furniture was all Louis XV and Louis XVI and of museum quality. The Louis XVI mahogany-and-bronze-doré desk once belonged to Queen Victoria.

Photographs by Henry S. Fullerton 3rd

LEFT AND BELOW: After the divorce, Mrs. Ford moved much of the furniture to New York, where McMillen rearranged it against slightly different backgrounds.

LEFT AND ABOVE: After her remarriage, the former Mrs. Ford moved to California, and in 1972 much of the furniture was sold at Sotheby's. As Mrs. Deane Johnson, she kept a New York *pied-à-terre*, which McMillen was asked to decorate in a way that would accommodate her new interest in Victoriana.

Photographs by Henry S. Fullerton 3rd and Michael Dunne

Saved from dereliction at the last moment, Rosedown Plantation in Louisiana (*below*) is now restored to its former glory and has become a showplace of the South. Much of the furniture, such as that found in the dining room (*below left*), came with the house, though it all had to be restored. The chairs are credited to Duncan Phyfe. A punkah over the table was reembroidered following its original eagle design by Audubon.

RIGHT: The painted chairs in the breakfast room were originally made for Brighton Pavilion but were never used there.

ABOVE: A curved staircase rises from the entrance hall. The chandelier always hung there; the bench is by Belter.

Photographs by Tom Leonard

BELOW: The attics of Rosedown were crammed with toys, many of which—like the rocking horse here—have found homes in refurbished bedrooms.

RIGHT: McMillen bought all the furniture for the music room but used the original antique materials to make new valances and trim new curtains.

ABOVE: The parlor is the most Victorian room in the house, with its carved furniture covered in red velvet. The valances are of pressed tin, and documents found in the house say that the fire screen was made by Martha Washington.

LEFT: The four-poster bed was one of many that were already in the house, but the rest of the furniture was bought for this room.

Photographs by Tom Leonard

207

BELOW: In another bedroom, there are French needlepoint chairs and an unusual swan cradle.

LEFT: The four-poster bed was one of many that were already in the house, but the rest of the furniture was bought for this room.

ABOVE: Stripping the wallpaper in the entrance hall revealed fragments of the original wallpaper. It was replaced with antique paper of the same pattern. The French table is by Lanier.

Photographs by Tom Leonard

And the house itself yielded clues. "The large pieces of furniture hadn't been moved for a hundred years," Ethel Smith says. "So when we finally moved them out of the house, we found they had protected the wallpaper behind them from fading. It still showed its true colors and patterns, and we were able to have Nancy McClelland reproduce them for us in New York. We could also tell what some of the fabrics had been like so we could reproduce those too for some upholstery and curtains."

There were also the delightful surprises that are a part of any restoration.

The punkah over the dining-room table still bore faint traces of a bird design and that, too, was painstakingly mapped out and duplicated. There was great excitement when it was discovered that the great naturalist and painter John James Audubon had tutored the daughters of the house at one time. It is almost certain that he did the original design which, when examined closely, was found to be an eagle.

A monumental Gothic bedroom suite that was being restored was discovered to have been made for Henry Clay in Clay's anticipation of his moving into the White House.

Everyone at McMillen became involved in Rosedown in one way or another as work progressed. "We were all very aware of the family who had lived there, and the house had a definite atmosphere of the old South that influenced us all," Ethel Smith explains.

"The thing I liked so much about Rosedown," Albert Hadley decided, "was the entireness of it all. There was the land being restored to grazing, the gardens being brought under control, the house being restored for family life. It was an historic house but it was also a domestic house."

But the Underwoods had never intended to live in Rosedown, and in 1962 it was opened to the public. Since then, it has become a regular stop on the house tours of the Mississippi delta.

Rosedown does evoke memories of the Turnbull family as was intended, but at least one visitor immediately saw the fine hand of McMillen behind the restoration.

"I was on a National Trust house tour a few years ago," Gregory B. Smith, for whom McMillen has decorated a dozen houses, says. "As soon as I walked into Rosedown, I knew McMillen *had* to have done it. There was nothing definite that I could point to that said so, but the McMillen touch was everywhere."

Design for a window treatment for Rosedown.

OVERLEAF: The restored Rosedown
Plantation in St. Francisville, Louisiana.

As the before and after pictures on
this and the next twelve pages show,
much of the furniture was found in
Rosedown but, like the house, was
sadly dilapidated. It was brought
back to life by a team of craftsmen
who worked for over a year in a
quonset hut set up on the grounds.
Black stripes outlining the ceiling
panels of the library entrance portico
(*right*) were painted in memory of
members of the family who had
fallen in battle, following local tradition. The bookcases in the library
were in the house; the chairs have
been re-covered. The portrait over the
mantel is of Edward Livingston, once
mayor of New York City and later a
member of the Louisiana legislature.
The wallpaper is a reproduction.
BELOW: The entrance hall as McMillen found it and (*below right*) as they
left it.

*All Rosedown post-restoration photo-
graphs are by Tom Leonard*

212

A pair of French consoles topped by
astral lamps flank the door from the
hall into the Victorian parlor. Beyond
is the library.

A fanciful *étagère-cum*-desk (*above*)
was restored with new mirrors. When
folded up, the writing shelf becomes
part of the paneling.

The lacquer-and-mother-of-pearl bed
in the room at left was a McMillen
discovery, but stenciled window
shades were in the house.

One of the many tasks undertaken was the restoration of decorative plasterwork (*right*).

A tall four-poster bed (*left and left above*) was moved with its twin to more suitable surroundings in a spacious, high-ceilinged room on the lower floor (*opposite page*).

Even in its most disheveled state, the curved mahogany staircase had considerable grace.

OPPOSITE PAGE: The upstairs hall. The doorway and wallpaper dado are duplicates of those in the lower hall.

OPPOSITE: A child's bedroom was turned into a breakfast room.

All of the rooms were given individual window treatments, and linens had to be specially made to fit the outsize beds. Existing furniture was supplemented with appropriate pieces, all from before 1835.

The parlor before and after restoration.

In homage to Audubon, bird cages
and bird prints became a prominent
decorative theme in the house.

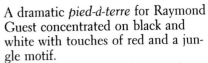

A dramatic *pied-à-terre* for Raymond Guest concentrated on black and white with touches of red and a jungle motif.

LEFT: The needlepoint hanging by Dom Robert came from the "Paris 1952" exhibit; the ottoman is made of monkey fur, the rug of zebra. The contemporary red-lacquered chest hides a bar, hi-fi, and TV.

ABOVE: Furniture was modern classic—Mies van der Rohe's leather "Barcelona" lounge chairs and Eero Saarinen's polypropylene "tulip" chairs and pedestal dining table.

LEFT: When it came to Mr. Guest's country house, however, tradition reigned, as shown by the entrance hall.

Photographs by Henry S. Fullerton 3rd

Even the best decorators do work they are not entirely happy with. ABOVE: This house was designed by the architect Philip Johnson. It was, according to McMillen, "a very cold space and we were asked to make it warmer and cozy." To this end, McMillen chose oversize furniture and a bright Jack Lenor Larsen print. But the result was not entirely successful. The traditional furniture jars with the architecture unless the room is populated by the large family that bought the house.

RIGHT: A room can look larger when sparsely furnished, but it can also merely look cold. The idea here was to provide coolness in the heat of Florida. The tiled floor and turquoise color scheme should have helped, but the mixing of traditionally patterned fabric with then-modern Swedish chairs and Italian branch lamps did not work.

Photograph by Henry S. Fullerton 3rd

This New York apartment was totally reconstructed from a warren of maids' rooms by McMillen. It is a coolly successful mix of traditional and contemporary.

TOP: In the bathroom, the tub was centered and given a "four-poster bed" effect through the use of tile and an end wall.

ABOVE: The kitchen and breakfast area are chocolate and white and streamlined—a popular combination in the 1960s.

LEFT AND ABOVE LEFT: In the living room, the eighteenth-century Italian chairs are covered in blue or brown suede, the sofas and slipper chairs in cotton. The rug is a dhurrie.

Photographs by Henry S. Fullerton 3rd

During the 1950s and 1960s McMillen decorated two Caribbean houses for William and Babe Paley. The first was in Jamaica (*this page*), the second in the Bahamas (*opposite page*). For most of her life, Babe Paley was renowned as an arbiter of taste in both fashion and design, and it was no mean compliment when she chose McMillen as her decorator. The emphasis in both houses was on natural materials that could stand up to subtropical heat.

Bedrooms like the one above were left open to the elements on one side and simply furnished. Shutters could be pulled across in bad weather.
TOP LEFT AND TOP RIGHT: The poolhouse in Jamaica. The loggia had a beige tiled floor and natural rattan furniture. Printed fabrics with bright bursts of red and orange were deliberately chosen to contrast with the pool and ocean beyond (*left*).

Photographs by Henry S. Fullerton 3rd

LEFT: In the Bahamas house, the dimensions of the living room were vast—the caryatids on either side of the fireplace are six feet high—so the furniture was massive in order to cope with the scale.

BELOW: As in Jamaica, the bedrooms were simply furnished with cotton prints and rattan and—in this one—decorated with wicker "trophies."

ABOVE: Shades of white in the atrium reflected the sun.

ABOVE: The Bahamas house was also planned to be open and airy, but its furnishings were more sophisticated than those used in Jamaica.

Photographs by Henry S. Fullerton 3rd

Three rooms: more than three different styles.

LEFT: A study that keeps its traditional backbone with a mahogany desk, captain's table, green leather couch, and sporting print is given a contemporary dressing by the cotton print used for the curtains and chairs.

BELOW: Modern brick-and-beam architecture takes on the aura of a centuries-old library, with books allowed to spill everywhere and comfortable seating.

ABOVE: An essay in Victoriana is saved from heaviness by calm oyster-colored walls and the restrained floral patterns of the sofas and rugs.

Photographs by Henry S. Fullerton 3rd

This small apartment was made to seem spacious by keeping the overall color white, punctuated by dashes of primary colors.

TOP: The mirrored wall in the living room slides back to reveal the bedroom (*above*). LEFT: The dining room had one wall mirrored and one lacquered charcoal-blue to produce an illusion of space and depth.

McMillen not only often designs interiors for several generations of one family; it also frequently operates laterally, working first for a couple when they are married and then separately for each of them when they divorce. These two pages illustrate a case in point. The beach house

When she moved into a city apartment, the lady wanted to retain a feeling of the country. So the living room (*above*) was painted a soft peach shade and flowers were introduced in the rug and the fabric.

TOP LEFT: To give the impression of a garden, the floor of the dining room was stained green, green silk curtains were hung at the windows, and a large-tulip-print fabric was used for the dining chairs. The mirror once belonged to William Odom.

(*above and top right*) was decorated for a couple. After their divorce, the wife moved to one apartment, the husband to another. McMillen decorated all. Perhaps predictably, the beach house was the most simply furnished. The Moroccan rug in the living room came with the house, comfortable sofas and chairs were covered in a Queen Anne's lace cotton print, and three Oriental marriage chests were used as coffee tables. The porch contained Brown Jordan garden furniture as well as a sweeping rattan couch that had its cushions covered in the same white cane-patterned vinyl used for the table top.

Photographs by Grigsby and Horst

The former husband's apartment reflects his bachelor status. The library (*top*) has suede-covered walls, upholstery fabric with large houndstooth checks, and brass-framed bookshelves. Three of his collection of Frederic Remington sculptures stand on the mantel, below a Charles M. Russell painting.

ABOVE RIGHT: In classical fashion, the entrance hall was left sparsely furnished, with a Tibetan rug the major decorative element. Another Remington stands on a table.

ABOVE LEFT: His bedroom has geometric-patterned curtains, cork-covered walls, and a tan leather bed and table unit.

Photographs by Horst and Otto Baitz

RIGHT: This massive beamed and vaulted living room with its huge stone fireplace was originally part of a stable.

ABOVE: Two walls, hung in printed cotton, have banquettes along them. "Arms" were made of cotton-covered sandbags.

RIGHT: The size of the room demanded overscaled furniture. In the center is a huge hexagonal Italian table.

This stark, modern house was designed as a setting for its owner's art collection. Rather than give it a bland, neutral interior, McMillen chose to use a quite strong yellow for the furnishings and rugs. Since the lines, like the architecture, were kept simple and blocky, the surprise of the color works.

Typical of architecture in the newly booming Florida of the 1930s was the aptly named Florida room. It was a loggia separated from the living room by a wall of glass and was open on its other three sides. However, since the time when such rooms were built, most have been enclosed on at least two sides, with the fourth given its own wall of sliding glass doors—from a design point of view, an ungainly result.

OPPOSITE PAGE AND ABOVE RIGHT: This room had gone through just such a transformation when its present owners bought it over twenty years ago and asked McMillen to decorate it—and the rest of the house—in three weeks. At that time McMillen suggested replacing the glass wall between the rooms with a solid one, but as there was not enough time, they compromised by hiding the glass behind curtains to make the room look like a room. The furnishings bought then are the same ones used today, but several years ago the owners asked McMillen to execute their original plan.

ABOVE LEFT: The result is a "proper" room, complete with decorative niche and green-lacquered doors.

RIGHT: The dining room, since it was a proper room to start with, needed no such changes. Although the lacquer table and pigskin-covered chairs came from the "Paris 1952" exhibition, the rest of the furnishings are traditional: a Louis XVI console, French Régence mirror, Spanish rug, and white Coromandel screen.

OPPOSITE: When Charles Revson bought former cosmetics rival Helena Rubinstein's New York apartment, McMillen designed the billiard room to his specifications, with the walls and ceiling covered with green felt and trimmed with brass nailheads. The table is antique.

Mr. Revson found the ballroom decaying and filled with glass cases that contained a collection of dolls. He decided to convert it back to its original purpose and insisted that McMillen produce something very formal and very French. After some hesitation, they did as he asked, designing all the architecture from scratch and bringing magnificence back to the badly dilapidated room. The walls were hung in green-and-white damask, the curtains were made of silk taffeta, and the upholstery was done in cut velvet. The crystal chandeliers and the candelabra on mahogany pedestals are modern reproductions. French windows with mirror panes were another sparkling addition to the room.

Collaborations between Tiffany & Co. and decorators to produce table settings on a theme—often something to do with breakfast—have long been a feature of the New York store. McMillen has participated in many, as this selection shows.

Natalie Davenport created a romantic breakfast setting (*top right*) in 1959, and in 1978 (*top left*) Ethel Smith and Betty Sherrill designed a luxurious supper table for gamblers whose luck was in.

CENTER RIGHT: The most recent, in 1981, was a sophisticated bachelor's dressing room/retreat designed by Jimmy Potucek.

BELOW: The earliest dates from 1958 and was designed by Betty Sherrill, who now has the S-shaped love seat, still in its original fabric, in her home.

Two teas were designed for Tiffany's: in 1961 by Albert Hadley (*right*) and in 1963 by Irene Walker (*far right*).

The 1950s also brought to McMillen a commission for one of the most important private residences in America.

When Mr. and Mrs. Henry Ford II bought a large Georgian-style red-brick mansion on the shores of Lake St. Clair in Grosse Pointe, Michigan, they asked McMillen to decorate it in its entirety.

The house, designed in the 1920s by the architect John Russell Pope, was to be a fitting background for Mr. Ford's superb collection of Impressionist art. The brief given McMillen was that every piece of furniture and every accessory was to be of the finest quality and mostly eighteenth-century French. Money was no object.

Marion Morgan, McMillen's expert in French and English eighteenth-century design, was in charge of the project, and Grace Fakes designed all the architectural detailing—moldings, cornices, *boiseries*, doors, and floors—that were not to be original.

Marion Morgan started by making several trips to Grosse Pointe, getting to know the house and the Fords. Floor plans were drawn, and Grace Fakes started sketching ideas for backgrounds.

Then Mrs. Morgan set off on the kind of shopping trip that every decorator must dream about.

The first stop was London. The library, Mr. Ford's study and bedroom, and a few other rooms were to be English rather than French, and with Anne Ford, herself a woman of great taste and a knowledgeable collector, Mrs. Morgan combed that city's top antique dealers.

It was the ultimate treasure hunt. Marion Morgan describes it: "We found a whole eighteenth-century paneled room for the library. The superb overmantel carving was by Grinling Gibbons, the Dutch master-woodcarver who settled in England and worked for both Charles II and Sir Christopher Wren. His work is still unsurpassed for its intricate detailing, grace and refinement.

"Then we found a pair of great Queen Anne lacquered secretaries at Partridge in Bond Street. We only needed one but the store would only sell them as a pair. Luckily, just before we left London, someone else came along who also wanted just one of them, so that worked out.

"But we weren't so lucky with an English chest of drawers we bought. After we got back to New York, we were told that the British government had decided that it was too important a piece to be allowed to be exported. It is now in the Victoria and Albert Museum in London.

"But we did get a Louis XVI *bureau plat* that had once been in Windsor Castle, a very rare set of twenty-four gilt Adam chairs (you don't usually find so large a set still intact) for the dining room, and more Adam furniture and an Adam-style rug for the entrance hall.

"Then we went to France for two weeks. I will never forget that. We had already found—in America—some Louis XV off-white and yellow paneling for the drawing room. It had belonged to Madame Jacques Balsan (the former Consuelo Vanderbilt and Duchess of Marlborough) and was in her house in Florida.

"But in Paris, we found antique *parquet de Versailles* flooring for that room, the Louis XV and Louis XVI furniture, and the Louis XIV Savonnerie rug. For the living room, we also bought mostly Louis XV chairs, though a few are Louis XVI.

"The living room also contained the Windsor Castle *bureau plat* and an ormolu decorated cabinet and a small console, both by Martin Carlin, the French cabinetmaker who did a lot of work for Madame du Barry for her famous château at Louveciennes. The console has a stamp on it indicating that it was made for Marie Antoinette's private apartments.

"The extraordinary thing about all the furniture bought for the Fords was its quality—really wonderful. Even the ladies' powder room had fine French pieces and a Louis XV screen.

"We also found antique paneling for the entrance hall and Mrs. Ford's second-floor sitting room, but Grace Fakes designed everything else.

"We used some antique fabrics on chairs but had others specially made. For example, the fabrics for the drawing-room curtains and Mrs. Ford's bed hangings and curtains were copied from old document prints and all hand-embroidered in Paris.

"I really think it was the finest house we've ever done."

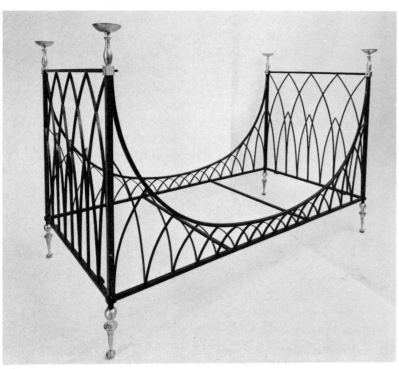

The room's starting point was a severe campaign bed (*above*) for which Grace Fakes created a fanciful canopy (*opposite page*).

The bedroom was decorated for the "Paris in New York" exhibition at McMillen in 1954 (see page 201).

OVERLEAF: The windows, curtains, and dressing table received a frothy treatment of net and lace.

That kind of decorating will probably never be repeated, even by McMillen. Today it is virtually impossible to find so much furniture of such quality on the market; the kind of handwork required for the embroidered fabrics is a rapidly dying art; and the cost of such furniture and specialized work would be prohibitive even for the wealthiest client.

When the Fords divorced in the 1960s, Henry Ford kept the paintings and Anne Ford the furniture. McMillen continued to work for Mrs. Ford when she moved to a New York apartment and then in her Los Angeles house when she remarried and became Mrs. Deane Johnson.

A recently completed New York *pied-à-terre* for the Johnsons shows how Anne Ford Johnson's tastes have changed over the years. Much of the French furniture was sold at auction in the 1970s, and the new apartment is definitely Victorian in feeling. McMillen, true to its creed of giving the client what she wants as long as it's the best, has changed along with her.

And why did the Fords ask McMillen to decorate their house? Well, it was really just a matter of keeping it all in the family. Anne Ford Johnson is one of the fourteen children of Mr. and Mrs. James McDonnell, for whom McMillen had worked in the 1930s. And later on, in the 1970s, when Charlotte Ford, Anne's daughter, wanted to try her wings as a designer, she learned the ropes at McMillen.

As soon as the Second World War had ended, Eleanor Brown resumed her regular trips to Europe—especially to France. Although she no longer had William Odom to guide her, by now she had her own network of contacts as well as his.

Always a Francophile and always ready to accept the new—if it was good—it wasn't long before she became convinced that although important ideas were coming from Italy, Scandinavia, and the Far East, the best new foreign design was coming from France. From that decision, it was but a short step to importing what Mrs. Brown liked best and introducing it through an exhibition at the firm's townhouse. In 1952, under the aegis of Betty Sherrill, two floors of the brownstone were given over to room settings—a living room, a dining room, and a self-contained bachelor's apartment—to show off the work of twenty-six young French artists, designers, and craftsmen. Called "Paris 1952," it was the first good look America had at French postwar design, and most experts thought it very good indeed.

The New Yorker published a comprehensive review: "Easily the best things . . . are the tapestries and rugs, all woven at the Aubusson factories in designs that bring an exciting new vigor to the old technique. Some of the lacquer work—on screens, table tops, and ornamental panels—is . . . just about as fine technically as such work can be, and there are various ceramics that are remarkable in both design and technique."

There was wrought-iron furniture by Gilbert Poillerat, including a dining table and a pair of *guéridons*, small occasional tables with inlaid marble tops supported by a sheaf of wrought-iron reeds. The *guéridons* were $350 each.

There was also a collection of leather furniture, designed by a group called Artistes Artisans Associés, which included a bookcase whose metal supporting rods were covered in black saddle leather stitched in white. It cost $575.

The New Yorker had this to say of a large leather desk and a commode: "The desk has a spacious elm top which is set on a frame of steel tubing covered with hand-stitched tan saddle leather, and three leather-covered drawers, which look like the top ends of a couple of magnificent Mark Cross suitcases, even to the regulation suitcase handles, for pulls. The commode is built in much the same way, with the same suitcaselike drawers. The desk is $500 and the commode $650. The luggage aspect isn't in the least eccentric, although it may sound as if it were; both pieces have a good deal of dignity, and would look very fine indeed in a man's room."

The New Yorker, however, did find one piece eccentric—a folding desk designed by Maxime Old. "Here, now," it exclaimed, "is something to which the decorators and dealers can apply—probably for the first time with any appropriateness—their favorite adjective, 'amusing'; whether you like it or not, the folding desk will almost certainly make you smile. The price tag, though, which says $1,500, will probably wipe the smile off in no time. This impressive thing is constructed like a combination drawing board and folding easel; a beautifully made and detachable box—it looks very much like an outsize paintbox of the kind that holds tubes of paint and a palette, and it has the same kind of handle—is mounted on the easel. One side of the box is covered in green leather and opens out to form a work surface, which is lined with red leather; the interior, also lined with red leather, is fitted with tiers of receptacles, in which letters, paper and all the paraphernalia of the writing table are kept in plain sight and easy reach—an obvious advantage. Leaving aside the *looks* of the desk, which are admittedly unconventional, there can be no two opinions about its meticulous craftsmanship, which is apparent in every line of its delicate pearwood frame and in the exquisite use of the red and green leathers. Indeed, it is this respect for materials and this concern for detail that help make the entire collection at McMillen so praiseworthy."

1960

If the 1950s were a decade of economic optimism and consumerism, the first half of the 1960s was a time of superoptimism and superconsumerism throughout the Western world.

In the United States the optimism was embodied in the election of John F. Kennedy as president and the almost immediate dubbing of his "court" as Camelot. In Britain, Prime Minister Harold Macmillan could tell his countrymen, "You've never had it so good," without being contradicted. France was under the autocratic but stabilizing leadership of Charles de Gaulle. Italy continued to have rapid changes of government but these were regarded as normal there, and the country was prosperous.

In the Western democracies, there were more people with more discretionary income than ever before. And especially in America, this was spent on cars, second homes, boats, and, now that the jet age was bringing the most far-flung places within the reach of the average person, on travel.

But primarily the 1960s were the decade of youth. The children born during the postwar baby boom were now entering their teens and twenties. These young people, born and brought up in affluence undreamed of by their parents, had no time for the traditions and conventions of the past. And now they had the spending power to make their opinions felt. The effects were enormous and, to many, shocking.

In such an atmosphere of change, it is not surprising that new ideas proliferated, nor that they now spread rapidly from one country to another.

For the first half of the decade, Britain led the way. The Beatles and the Rolling Stones became universal youth heroes, and London's Kings Road and Carnaby Street were regarded internationally as the centers of style.

And what a style. Like the young people who so enthusiastically followed it, it was brash, colorful, noisy, and for *now*. Things were not designed to last, for a world that was going to be blown up tomorrow.

American youth seemed to agree, and London became a mecca from which they returned to spread the new gospel of "Pop"—pop music, pop art, pop fashion, and pop design.

As in all manifestations of "Pop," pop design had to be fun, bright, up-to-the-minute, and readily available. And, thanks to technological advances, all this—and more—was suddenly possible.

alie Davenport decorated this li-
ry for herself. Since it gets a lot of
 from both south- and east-facing
dows, the walls were painted a
p blue to absorb some of the
e.

tograph by Henry S. Fullerton 3rd

At the end of the 1950s a new plastic, polypropylene, had been discovered, and now that it had been developed commercially, it revolutionized furniture design. Unlike the other plastics already on the market, polypropylene was strong enough not to need reinforcement by either metal or fiberglass. Furniture made of this new material could be mass-produced easily by injection molding, and because it could stand on its own, it could also be produced cheaply—for about half the cost of a reinforced-plastic piece. It was also a plastic that took strong colors well, and it was almost impossible to chip or stain it.

Another brand-new element that quickly captured the imagination of everyone was the advent of the space race. As America pushed closer and closer to the moon and astronauts joined the ranks of the new heroes, there was a rapid adoption of many of the stylistic trimmings of space technology in both fashion and the home.

Kitchens were designed in emulation of futuristic space-station galleys. For many people, beds were not complete without an accompanying panel of push buttons and switches that by remote control regulated the opening and closing of curtains, the dimming and brightening of lights, and the operation of a television and stereo system. These last two—television and stereo—were now essential components in every self-respecting home, redesigned to be as streamlined and spacecraftlike as possible, and proudly displayed as part of the decor rather than hidden behind flush cabinetry.

At the same time, low-cost foam rubber and the new stretch-jersey upholstery fabrics appeared, and furniture designers in search of the new—as most of them were—rapidly embraced them in an attempt to satisfy the needs for self-expression and unconventionality that seemed common to everyone under thirty.

The new plastics, foam rubber, and stretch fabrics could all be utilized for futuristic effects—and sometimes shock. Clear plastic Lucite chairs or chaises, foam-rubber blocks carved into abstract forms and covered with brightly colored fabric, and shiny white vinyl or metallic wallpapers immediately suggested the twenty-first century.

These experiments in design inevitably led to some fads—such as furniture of disposable paper and inflatable plastic—but they also changed the serious side of design. For the youth movement was not entirely frivolous. In its rebellion against the status quo of "quiet good taste," it produced a new way of living and looking at life that we now take for granted.

The lead was taken by Italian designers. The postwar years in Italy had seen the start of a design renaissance that now came into its own. The best of the young Italian designers, centered around Milan, placed a high premium on style, and it was their inventive work that produced the best examples of what could be done with the new synthetics. Some of their designs produced high style at high cost, but many led to the first sophisticated modular furnishings that were both mass-produced and low-cost. Their leaders were Joe Colombo, Vico Magistretti, Mario Bellini, and Tobia and Afra Scarpa—all names that still rank high in the design world.

It was Italian designers who really brought class to plastic and foam rubber and, indeed, caused their work with these materials to be as highly regarded as the much more luxurious and expensive designs they were creating from marble, leather, and wood.

Both the British "Pop" explosion and the Italian design renaissance quickly traveled to the United States. But America made its own vital contribution to the maelstrom of new design that shaped the decade.

The exuberance of youth, the "off with the old, on with the new" philosophy, was perhaps best illustrated by the new generation of American "Pop" artists such as Roy Lichtenstein, Claes Oldenburg, Jasper Johns, and Andy Warhol, and abstract painters such as Mark di Suvero, Ellsworth Kelly, Frank Stella, and Morris Louis, who came to be known as "the New York School."

Their art had a direct impact on interior design. First of all, almost everyone could afford the new art. Because their works were experimental and unorthodox, at the beginning originals cost a few thousand dollars at most and many were in the hundreds. And if originals were beyond your budget, these same artists' work could be bought as prints and posters.

The traditional way of using paintings as cultural accessories didn't work with this new art. Because most of these canvases and sculptures were so large and their images so demanding, they became the focus of attention in a room. Walls were painted white to accommodate them and furniture became dramatically more colorful to complement the colors and shapes of the artwork.

Other influences were at work, too. International Modernism, which by the 1950s had segued into Contemporary, reemerged in a purer form much closer to its Bauhaus roots. It really wasn't surprising that the influence of the Bauhaus should return, especially in America. After all, wherever they had trained, most young American architects had by now been directly affected by it, for most of its leaders had come to the United States when they fled Nazism in the late 1930s. Walter Gropius had been made head of the Harvard School of Architecture in 1937 and Marcel Breuer had also taught there. Mies van der Rohe had

Strong prints and stronger colors
started to predominate in the 1960s.
Here, the color scheme was bright
red, yellow, and orange.

been dean of architecture at the Armour Institute in Chicago. Two other leaders of the Bauhaus, Laszlo Moholy-Nagy and Josef Albers, had also instilled into students their ethic of functionalism at institutes they founded (Moholy-Nagy in Chicago and Albers in North Carolina). Their influence had been so great, in fact, that by the 1960s it was difficult to find an architect or architecture department that didn't wholeheartedly believe in the house as a machine for living.

In interiors, too, the early Bauhaus designs now returned, but this time as status symbols. As Tom Wolfe wrote in 1981 in an article in *Harpers:*

> *Every young architect's apartment, and every architecture student's room, was that box and that shrine. And in that shrine was always*

the same icon. I can still see it. The living room would be a mean little space on the backside of a walkup tenement. The couch would be a mattress on top of a flush door supported by bricks and covered with a piece of monk's cloth. There would be more monk's cloth used as curtains and on the floor would be a sisal rug that left corduroy ribs on the bottoms of your feet in the morning. The place would be lit by clamp-on heat lamps with half-globe aluminum reflectors and ordinary bulbs replacing the heat bulbs. At one end of the rug, there it would be . . . the Barcelona chair. Mies had designed it for his German Pavilion at the Barcelona Exposition of 1929. The Platonic ideal of chair it was, pure Worker Housing leather and stainless steel, the

Photographs by Henry S. Fullerton 3rd

Painted furniture became very popular. In this room, the deep pastels used in the paisley-print slipcovers—pink, yellow, and mauve—were painted onto wood and wicker furniture.

most perfect piece of furniture design in the twentieth century. The Barcelona chair commanded the staggering price of $550, however, and that was wholesale. When you saw that holy object on the sisal rug, you knew you were in a household where a fledgling architect and his young wife had sacrificed everything to bring the symbol of the godly mission into their home. Five hundred and fifty dollars! She had even given up the diaper service and was doing the diapers by hand. It got to the point where, if I saw a Barcelona chair, no matter where, I immediately—in the classic stimulus-response bond—smelled diapers gone high.

But if they already had the chair, why was she still doing the diapers by hand? Because one chair was only halfway to Mecca. Mies always used them in pairs. The state of grace, the Radiant City, was two Barcelona chairs, one on either side of the sisal rug, before the flush-door couch, under the light of the heat-lamp reflectors.

Nonarchitects might not go in for such sacrifices, but they were seduced, too. The architectural opening up of the home that had taken place in the 1950s led, in the 1960s, to the completely open-plan room with the division of functions—sitting, working, dining—

250

marked only by a step up or down, a platform, or a sunken seating area.

Space was still fluid, but layouts were less flexible and were best served by furniture that had more sharply etched lines than the "organic" designs of the previous decade. The austerity of shape and materials—metal, leather, and glass—of the Bauhaus designs worked well in these more disciplined settings as they also did when seen against white walls and the new pop and abstract art.

Thus the 1920s designs of Mies van der Rohe, Marcel Breuer, and Le Corbusier returned as modern classics, as much revered by some as a Louis XVI chair was by others.

However, design and desires in the 1960s were nothing if not varied. Running parallel to the cult of the new was a strong vein of nostalgia. In the 1930s there had been an equally strong move back to the romantic past in decoration, partly because of the strong impact of Streamlined Moderne, which was itself a reaction to Art Nouveau.

Now there were the same yearnings for the past. But this time, Art Nouveau *was* the past. Triggered partly by a 1960 exhibition of Art Nouveau at New York's Museum of Modern Art, there was an upsurge of interest in William Morris's swirling, sensuous designs for wallpapers and fabrics, Thonet's bentwood chairs were hunted down in junkshops, and the elaborate lamps of Louis Tiffany, which had been given away by previous owners or were gathering dust in attics, now became collectors' items.

But by 1968, the carefree mood was changing. Below the glitter and gaiety of "Swinging London," undercurrents of economic woes to come were beginning to be felt. In France, students at the Sorbonne rioted, put up the barricades, and fought the police for weeks. In Italy, there were the first stirrings of the extreme left and talk of anarchy and terrorism.

But it was in the United States that the rose-colored spectacles were changing hue most radically. As the build-up of men in Vietnam and the death toll of young Americans there accelerated, disillusionment in the American Dream—already hit hard three times by the assassinations of John and Robert Kennedy and Martin Luther King—increased. Young people became hippies, flower children, or just "dropped out" into a rebellious counterculture, and although the home and its furnishings were far from their thoughts, they did influence both.

People who appreciated this casual style of living found that they could react against materialism in their own homes by using piles of pillows and cushions instead of chairs, using a bed instead of a sofa, covering everything in roughly woven, multipatterned In-

A riot of pattern and color in a child's room. The walls were covered in green-and-white gingham checks; the upholstery fabric was red, yellow, and orange; and the rug was in shades of blue with white.

dian fabrics, and burning incense. The result was ethnic, as desired, but generally naïve. It did, however, help spur an interest in the natural and the handmade that would really take off, for other reasons, in the 1970s.

But if political disillusionment was setting in at the end of the 1960s, economically the good life continued. Great thought was being given to how we were going to spend the increased leisure time that—thanks to advanced technology and automation inside and outside the home—all of us would have.

The winds of change of the 1960s blew everywhere in interior design, but when they arrived at McMillen, they became a gentle breeze. Eleanor Brown did not resist the new but she did object to fads. Her keen editor's eye, undimmed although she was now in her seventies, was quick to spot the difference between the new and the novel. The latter never stood a chance in the townhouse on East 55th Street.

HERE AND ON THE NEXT TWO PAGES:
Tradition still reigned in this gun
room (and it has lasted: see page
189), which was decorated by
McMillen with dark green walls and
a white linen fabric with a blue-and-
green crewel design.

The company continued its elegant, timeless interiors which appealed to most of its clientele, but the
firm did react positively to some of the new trends—
especially the advent of more color. Strong, clear
greens, yellows, corals, and blues started to appear in
the interiors they were designing all over the country.

As might be expected, Mrs. Brown also cham-
pioned the new importance of art and had no objec-
tion to the new synthetics if they fulfilled a need that
a natural fiber couldn't meet.

McMillen changed, but subtly. By the late 1970s
many people found themselves with "modern" interiors that had their date clearly stamped on them and

therefore already looked out-of-date. McMillen's clients, however, found themselves with rooms that still
looked fresh.

This ability to be up-to-date but not *of* a date was
recognized by *House & Garden,* America's leading
shelter magazine. McMillen interiors were featured in
House & Garden no fewer than eighteen times during
the 1960s, seven times on its cover—the highest compliment in an increasingly competitive interior-design
world.

For interior design was now a full-fledged profession. The Establishment—McMillen, "Sister" Parish, Billy Baldwin, and Dorothy Draper—were now

challenged by Michael Taylor, John Dickinson, and Anthony Hail, all based on the West Coast but not averse to making forays east. In New York, Angelo Donghia and Mario Buatta were making their names.

There was also the growing influence of such architects as Richard Meier, Paul Rudolph, Louis Kahn, and Philip Johnson to contend with. For these architects, it was not enough to design the building; they also wanted to plan all its furnishings following their International Modernist precepts.

In addition, it was becoming obvious that furnishing great houses, like the Henry Fords', with the finest period furniture was rapidly becoming a thing of the past. Very little was on the market and what came up was increasingly expensive, even for the wealthiest.

None of these changes directly influenced McMillen in the 1960s. Their interiors reflected the trends in that they became more colorful and simplified, and their clients—who were still steadily increasing in number—might want to show off a fine

contemporary art collection or add some of the classic modern furniture to their homes, but they were not interested in ethnic authenticity or "Pop" plastic.

There were no great houses to restore, like Rosedown, or to create, like the Fords', for McMillen in the 1960s, but there were great challenges.

During the Kennedy administration, Jacqueline Kennedy organized a committee to renovate Blair House, the nation's official guest house in Washington, D.C. The renovation and refurbishing was all paid for by private subscription but the decorating was turned over to professionals.

McMillen was asked to decorate six rooms: the president's office (his own room when he is at Blair House); the Lincoln Room (the entrance hall where guests are welcomed on arrival); the dining room; the Blair-Lee double drawing room (where most entertaining takes place); the King's Bedroom (reserved for heads of state); and the Prime Minister's Room (an adjoining sitting room).

"Mrs. Brown and I went down to Washington together," Betty Sherrill recalls. "I walked in there and said, 'You mean our presidents stayed here and this is where we put the Queen of England?' There wasn't an ashtray that wasn't terrible. We bought everything except, I think, the dining-room chairs." No attempt was made to restore the house to any particular period but the McMillen rooms, as might be expected, are comfortable, gracious, and scholarly.

Later on, when the Lyndon Johnsons moved into the White House, McMillen decorated their private quarters. "We were never allowed to photograph that," Betty Sherrill regrets, but Ethel Smith, who worked on the rooms, describes them: "Mrs. Johnson didn't change the dining room at all. But we made the sitting room a very pretty yellow and white with coral. Mrs. Johnson's bedroom was hung with coral watered silk, with a canopy bed hung with the same fabric. Her little sitting room next to it had a chinoiserie 'tree of life' paper on the walls and on the top floor we made a little Texas hideaway for Luci, complete with barbecue."

Also in Washington, a challenge of a different kind was the work McMillen did for Mrs. Marjorie Merriweather Post, the General Foods heiress. "She lived like a Russian tsarina," Tom Buckley, who worked on the designs with Grace Fakes, says. "Troops of servants, unending houses, unending apartments. She got exactly what she wanted with a flick of her wrist. She had a spy system that was so efficient she knew exactly what was going on in all of her houses all over the country and halfway around the world and she also knew everything that was happening at General Foods.

"She was very fair. If you told her the truth, no matter how bad it was, she would forgive you anything. Lie to her and you were out.

"She lived in a grandeur that was unbelievable for the twentieth century. I remember Marion Morgan and me taking a bench that had belonged to Marie Antoinette down to her. She took one look at it and said, 'Well, I guess I have to have it.' Then Marion saw something in London that had belonged to one of the tsars and she brought a picture of it back to show Mrs. Post.

"The piece cost $13,000 then—that would be about $50,000 now. 'Well, I guess I'd better have it,' she said. 'You, young man, go upstairs and send a cable.'"

So far, she sounds like the ideal client. But John Drews remembers that "you always had to do four or five of everything. If it was a design for a window, you'd send Mrs. Post the first three or four and it didn't matter how good they were, they'd come back with 'ugly' or 'vulgar' scrawled across them. So you'd send down three more and the last one would be 'beautiful.' It was a habit with her. I think Tom Buckley framed one of the 'uglier,' 'vulgar' ones.

"Also, a lot of her furniture was copied. She copied a French chair so that it could have a thing to pull out for drinks. Everything had to have a gimmick or something going on with it. If it was a bed table it had sixteen buttons to call the maids and all kinds of things built into it but it was all in Louis XVI style. But the house had a lot of beautiful things—a lot of them bought by McMillen."

In New York, McMillen was asked to decorate the offices of Charles Revson, the cosmetics tsar. "Mrs. Brown said no to that," Betty Sherrill recalls. "We were very busy, and she knew what kind of taste he had—gilt and red velvet. Then he said, 'What about my house?' and she said no to that too. Finally, he said 'What about my ballroom?' and Mrs. Brown thought and said, 'We haven't done a ballroom for a while, we'll do that.'"

John Drews, who once again was to work on the

The dining room of Blair House.

designs with Grace Fakes, remembers Mr. Revson's first visit to McMillen. "He drove up in his limousine with his entourage, came in and said he could give us five minutes and where was the old lady. We all cringed.

"Then, he wanted us to do the billiard room. He sent me off to see a billiard room in one of his friends' houses that he wanted me to copy. It was not very good—it looked like a men's locker room basically—and I told him so and also that it wasn't really fair to ask one designer to copy the work of another, even if it was good. He absolutely blew up, banged his fist on the table and yelled, 'Everybody copies. How do you think I got where I am today? We all copy from each other.'

"I tried to take the basic ideas and do them our way, but he rejected that and eventually we gave him what he wanted—lots of green felt and plaid carpet. When it was finished, Mr. Revson came to see it, looked at me, and said, 'Now, John, tell me this isn't pretty.' It was, because we had used better materials, added mahogany wainscoting and large brass nailheads for detail. Mr. Revson enjoyed forcing you to do things his way. He liked that kind of power over people."

The ballroom also was a compromise, but one that turned out well. Ben Flowers, a decorator who had just joined McMillen, remembers: "We all worked a long time on the designs and Mrs. Brown found a marvelous set of antique Chinese panels for the walls. We submitted what we thought was a truly beautiful scheme and we were all very proud of it. He turned it down flat. He wanted something much more grand with damask and gold and columns. And that's eventually what he got—it was much more formal and French than we had wanted—but toned down."

Betty Sherrill had problems of a different kind with Charles Revson. "I invited him for dinner one evening, and I almost starved. He was hung up on high cholesterol and when he found out that my level was quite high, he looked at everything my cook sent up and ordered it taken away if it contained any meat or had a sauce. And away it went. I tried telling him my doctor wasn't worried about me, but all that did was make him demand that I get another doctor.

"However, we ended up with a beautiful ballroom, although I don't think he ever held a ball there."

But these special projects and the still increasing number of clients meant that, once more, Eleanor Brown had to expand McMillen. At the beginning of the 1960s, the senior decorating and design staff consisted of Mrs. Brown, Grace Fakes, Ethel Smith, Marion Morgan, Betty Sherrill, Natalie Davenport, Irene Walker, Tom Buckley, and Albert Hadley. During the course of the decade, Grace Fakes retired, Albert Hadley left to go into partnership with "Sister" Parish, and at the end of 1969 Tom Buckley left to start his own firm in Los Angeles. But Kevin McNamara, John Drews, Mary Louise Guertler, Alexandra Stoddard, Fred Cannon, and Ben Flowers were hired. Martha Snyder retired as business manager, to be replaced by the equally firm Irene Booth. Add to these the backup staff of secretaries, bookkeepers, and shipping clerks, and McMillen was by far the largest private decorating firm in the country, with a staff approaching forty. The townhouse was about as full as it could be.

This large staff of course meant a large overhead. Looking ahead, Eleanor Brown and other senior members of the staff such as Betty Sherrill became less and less convinced that purely private work would be able to support the company in the future. It was not so much that they saw an economic recession ahead but they did see increased labor costs, more competition within the profession, and a growing tendency for potential clients to do their own decorating.

The other side of interior design is contract work—designing offices, boardrooms, and cafeterias—for corporations. McMillen had always done some of this work, but mostly for corporations whose executives they had worked for privately. Now, however, a formal contract department was set up under John Drews and Tom Buckley, and the firm began actively wooing banks, clubs, hotels, and other businesses.

The contract department was not to get into really high gear until the 1970s, but in the 1960s McMillen landed contracts from NBC in New York, the Ritz Carlton Hotel in Boston, the Chevy Chase Club in Maryland, and the River Oaks Club in Houston.

This corporate work was varied. Some clients wanted to exude stability and solid conservatism, and therefore wanted even the most modern offices decorated with traditional moldings, cornices, and antique furniture—the kind of interior that McMillen was especially noted for.

But others wanted the status look of International Modernism with its leather and steel furniture and stark walls. McMillen provided this too, although gentling it with color and accessories whenever possible. But it wasn't until 1972 when Luis Rey, today a vice-president, joined the firm, that it really achieved expertise in the modern idiom.

Still, as the 1960s ended and Eleanor Brown prepared to celebrate her eightieth birthday, McMillen, like most of America, was riding a wave of economic success.

One-half of the double drawing room at Blair House, the official guesthouse for heads of state visiting Washing- ton. The opposite end of the room is its almost identical twin.

Photograph by Ernest Beadle

When Blair House was refurbished during the Kennedy administration, McMillen was asked to do six of the rooms.

ABOVE AND PREVIOUS PAGE: The furnishings of the double drawing room (donated by the Honorable Douglas Dillon) point up the absolute symmetry of the room. The mantels are Adam, as are the mirrors; the rugs are Ushaks, while the wallpaper is eighteenth-century Chinese. All the furniture is eighteenth-century English and of museum quality.

LEFT: The reception room, donated by Winthrop Aldrich, is hung in silk damask. Again, all the furniture is antique, although the rug is a modern reproduction.

Photographs by Ernest Beadle

ABOVE: The dining room was the only room for which appropriate furniture already existed. Mrs. Edgar Garbisch donated the dinner service of blue-and-white Lowestoft china and Eleanor Brown gave the mirror.

RIGHT: Mrs. Angier Biddle Duke and Mrs. Harcourt Amory asked that the room for which they were to donate furniture, the King's Bedroom, be Early American in style. It contains a fine Early American maple four-poster bed, although the needlepoint rug is modern. One regal touch: a needlepoint lion on a cushion.

Photographs by Ernest Beadle

Although McMillen has always been renowned for its use of custom designs and custom-made materials, it has not limited itself to them. Indeed, when asked, McMillen's designers can work with only mass-produced home furnishings and fabrics, as they showed in 1969, when Celanese Corporation, one of the giants of the synthetic-fiber industry, asked them to do just that. The brief: Furnish a nineteenth-century New York townhouse that was to serve as the company's showroom. Working for a theoretical Celanese family—an executive, his wife, and their two teenage children—McMillen used light, bright colors to visually enlarge the small rooms.

ABOVE: In the children's bathroom, old fixtures were retained, with white painted pipes left exposed against bright orange walls.

ABOVE RIGHT: In the library, moldings were picked out in white and walls covered in tobacco-colored fabric with braid in a geometric design based on one in the Lincoln Room at the White House (the New York house was built by Robert Todd Lincoln, son of the president).

RIGHT: The dining-room walls were covered in a monochrome checkerboard damask accented by the McMillen hallmark—a panel of smoked-glass mirrors.

Photographs by Grigsby

A bedroom/study for a teenage boy
has both ample room for the tools of
schoolwork and a hard-to-harm floor
for play.

Photograph by Henry S. Fullerton 3rd

Lacquer and shine, whether dark or light, came into their own in the 1970s, always with dramatic effect. RIGHT: Here, out-and-out shine is reduced to a minimal presence—a sculpture by Steve Porter over the fireplace. The furniture reflects another stylistic trend of the 1970s: the use of wicker and rattan.

BELOW: To get the desired effect in this living room, the walls were given seven coats of paint and four of clear lacquer.

ABOVE: A white-and-silver dining room with navy-blue accents makes a cool contrast to the red glow from the adjoining living room.
LEFT: A red-on-red living room has lacquered walls and table and a red-and-white dhurrie rug. The painting is by Larry Zox.

Photographs by Horst and Tom Yee

LEFT: Deep purple with bright red as an accent looks quieter than it sounds when used for a library in a sunny clime.

ABOVE: A bold chintz and a Coromandel screen are smartly set off by walls lacquered a deep apricot.
RIGHT: Brown, black, and white geometric paper has a soft shine that complements the deep honey color of a Biedermeier bed.

Photographs by Michael Dunne

This living room (*right*) and library (*below right*) are in the same apartment building as those below, which were originally identical. They illustrate what can be done by the same decorators with the same architecture for different clients who have differing tastes. The rooms on the right are traditional and urbane; those on the left are also traditional but have the country feel the clients asked for. Because the library below doubles as

a guest room, the clients did not want the room to be wall-to-wall books, and space for the overflow had to be made in the living room. The architectural differences in the rooms—all designed by McMillen— meet these individual needs in the same way that the completely different decorative elements reflect the personality of each client.

Photographs by Michael Dunne

Mrs. Marjorie Merriweather Post "lived like a Russian tsarina" in several houses. This is the opulent octagonal breakfast room in one of them. Mirrored walls are framed by gilt *treillage* and reflect a table set with Sèvres china that was made in 1792 for Prince Louis de Rohan. The chandelier was originally made for the Palace of Pavlovsk near Leningrad.

Photograph by Horst

In one art-dominated apartment, furnishings are kept neutral but shapes are softened. The collection includes (*top right*) panels by Louise Nevelson, chrome sculpture by Eduardo Paolozzi, and a canvas by Morris Louis, along with such ancient art as a very rare Colima terra-cotta circle and two small fourth-century A.D. Mayan reliefs. But the emphasis is on modern masters, and there are other paintings by Jean Dubuffet (*top left*), Jack Youngerman (*above right*), and Frank Stella and Roy Lichtenstein (*above left*).

Photographs by Horst

This duplex belonged to the owner of an art gallery and was intended to be a contemporary background for frequently changed paintings and sculpture. McMillen designed an interior that was—as the client requested—neutral but, at the same time, high-style.

BELOW: The restraint of the design gives the only antique furniture—a set of fine Regency dining chairs—added impact.

ABOVE: The stairs connecting the levels of the duplex were made an important decorative element by their being carpeted in a pattern that evokes the design of the African mask at the foot of the staircase.

LEFT AND LEFT ABOVE: White predominates, but the pale-on-pale scheme is given interest with varying textures—ceramic tiles on floors, chairs of rattan or suede, textured linen covering sofas and lacquered onto coffee and end tables.

This beach house, perched on a dune, was furnished for a look of simplicity and for easy maintenance. The walls are painted wood; the floors are covered with sisal matting and dhurrie rugs and the furniture with hard-wearing canvas duck. The palette is neutral, with splashes of color coming from cushions and a David Hockney painting.

Photographs by Horst

For clients whose taste was evolving from the traditional in one house (*top right*) to the contemporary in another, McMillen designed this kitchen/dining area (*top left*) and two bathrooms for the new house. In style, the dining area is transitional, with a traditional rug, chairs, and door moldings, but it adjoins a sleekly modern kitchen and spiral staircase. The table of burled wood and wrought iron bridges the stylistic gap.

ABOVE LEFT: The guest bathroom is uncompromisingly contemporary. The master bathroom (*above right*), with its patterned walls and circular double sink unit, is softly so.

McMillen's portfolio of corporate clients has increased rapidly in the last twenty years to the point that they now account for 50 percent of McMillen's business. The stylistic variety of McMillen's work for these clients is as broad as that of their residential work, although in corporate design such things as lighting, flow patterns, and harder use make increased demands. Corporate design also means that the decorator is usually working with a committee rather than with an individual. But the scope is still wide, as is shown on these pages.

On this page, four reception areas— the first and all-important impression a company makes on visitors.

TOP LEFT: For a dramatic introduction to a large investment bank, black leather walls set off Italian "Saratoga" chairs.

ABOVE: A radio station acquired instant chic with a partition of brightly painted slats and Eero Saarinen's "tulip" chairs and pedestal tables.

TOP RIGHT: For the huge reception area of a large oil company, the floors and a curved elevator wall are of granite. Other walls are of either glass or bronze panels. The continuous-seating system designed by McMillen is covered in green leather and raised on a granite platform above green

carpeting. Coffee tables are bronze cylinders. The reception desk has space for one receptionist and two guards.

ABOVE: A medium-sized oil company contented itself with a travertine floor and black metal-strip ceiling as a

background for an antique Tibetan rug, modern glass-and-chrome table, and Ward Bennett "tub" chairs.

Photographs by Michael Dunne and Otto Baitz

ABOVE RIGHT: The main stairway in an investment bank is suitably opulent, with its heavy carpeting and bronze rails and panels.
ABOVE LEFT: A subsidiary staircase at the same firm was a standard fire escape that has been improved by the addition of carpeting, wall covering, and prints.

Banquettes are used to subdivide two large cafeterias into more intimate spaces. In one (*top right*), oak strips and butcher-block tabletops add warmth, as do wall hangings with images of assorted vegetables. In the other (*center left*), quarry tile is used for walls and banquettes although the floor is carpeted. The "art" is a Jack

Lenor Larsen fabric stretched over frames. In both, the chairs are Breuer's "Cesca" design, with differently upholstered backs and seats.

Photographs by Otto Baitz and Michael Dunne

RIGHT: The company that asked for an office on a budget got this smart interior.

ABOVE: With a much larger budget, a corporate dining room got a custom-made table, traditional furniture, and hand-painted murals.

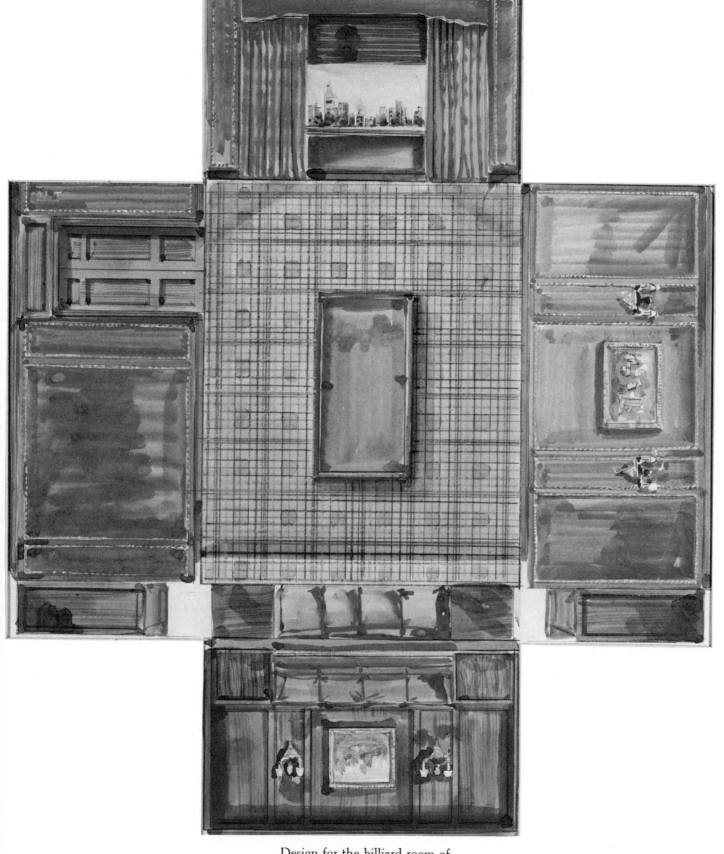

Design for the billiard room of
Charles Revson.

OVERLEAF: Fine French Furniture
was still being bought and given the
finest of settings: here, striéed paneled walls and hand-appliquéd curtains.

Photograph by Henry S. Fullerton 3rd

Betty Ford (*shown at left*) and Betty Sherrill looking over the table settings for the state dinner held at the White House in 1976 for Queen Elizabeth.

We are still so close to the 1970s that it is difficult to appraise them objectively. The individualism of the 1960s continued, but it gradually changed from the innocence of "doing your own thing" to the cynicism of the "Me Generation."

The mounting protests over the war in Vietnam and the Watergate scandal forced Americans to reappraise their moral values; at the same time, their material values were tested by the dramatic rise in oil prices decreed in 1973 by the newly formed Organization of Petroleum Exporting Countries (OPEC).

But at the beginning, the future looked relatively carefree. Automation and the computer were going to liberate everyone, from the housewife to the white-collar worker. Electronic devices for the home abounded, from the microwave oven to the centrally installed vacuum system. The emphasis was on maintenance-free materials.

There were other changes within the home, many of them continuations of the eclecticism of the 1960s. The experimental work with new materials in that decade was consolidated in the 1970s. There was nothing that, strictly speaking, could be called new, but the boundaries of what constituted "good taste" had never been wider.

Decoratively, the interest in space-age technology and its trappings developed into a style dubbed Minimalism. Its aesthetic decrees that there should be nothing that is superfluous; everything should be pared down to essentials. Classically, walls are plain, painted shiny white. Platforms to support various room functions are built in, and all is covered by gray industrial carpeting. Lighting—track, spot, and recessed—is important and often used to set a mood. A few carefully chosen objects, carefully lit, are the only relief apart from, occasionally, a splash of red.

Later on in the decade, Minimalism was to beget High Tech, in which purely industrial articles—steel framing, metal subway ventilation grids, hospital trolleys, restaurant ranges, and factory lights—were used instead of sheetrock, wood flooring, drinks carts, and conventional cooking and lighting equipment. In both Minimal and High Tech interiors, windows had either plain vertical blinds or no covering at all.

Once again the most stylish of contemporary furniture came from Italy. Throughout the 1970s, Italian designers held on to their lead in mass-producing high-quality plastic and fiberglass furniture at reasonable prices. Now they also expanded the luxury end of the market. Using leather, glass, marble, and wood in simple but sensuous and tactile ways, they produced a range of furniture that is universally acknowledged to be the most exciting contribution to interior design in the last ten years and made Milan the center of the design world. Colombo, Magistretti, the Scarpas, Bellini, and now Gae Aulenti and Cini Boeri came to stand alongside the Bauhaus greats—Mies, Breuer, Le Corbusier—in prestige.

But for those who didn't want to be either Minimalist or Modern, there was no shortage of alternatives. Then why use a decorator? The 1970s were the decade of the shelter magazine—*House & Garden, House Beautiful, Architectural Digest, American Home.* All were full of pictures of rooms that could be copied (sometimes with tips on how to do it) or adapted. So more and more people turned to do-it-yourself decorating. In place of professional treatments, sheets in a myriad of colors and "designer" patterns were shirred on walls, hung as curtains, made into slipcovers, or draped from ceilings, tent-fashion.

Well-designed plastic furniture was cheap; wicker returned as an inexpensive alternative to upholstery; and carpet-covered plywood platforms and blocks of foam covered in sheet fabrics substituted for sofas and beds.

After two decades of traveling the world, financed by a strong dollar, many Americans had collected—or at least accumulated—an assortment of treasures and mementos. Now the African masks were hung as though they were Picassos and the pre-Columbian figures lit as though they were Rodins. In many cases, the artifacts became the furnishings of a room. Thai brass drums were used as coffee tables; African baskets held magazines.

Then, in the middle of the decade, American relations with China were "normalized" and that country's influence became all-pervasive. Chinese lacquer, porcelain, bamboo furnishings, silks, and art were avidly sought. If they were new, they were cheap; if they were old, they were chic.

The last twelve years have also been a time of galloping nostalgia. The return of Art Nouveau led directly to a revival of Art Deco, and by 1980 there was a small but potentially potent reawakening of interest in 1950s Contemporary.

But the decorating world wasn't limited to foreign art and artifacts for its accessories and furniture. America was now found to have a rich store of history of its own.

As the Bicentennial approached in 1976, there was a swelling of a new pride in, and appreciation of,

Americana. Shaker furniture, old patchwork quilts, Indian rugs, folk art, pewter, and pressed glass were all sought after and became the nucleus of new collections.

But the decade was pulled up, midstream, by the energy crunch. The economic effects were immediate, and nowhere were they felt more rapidly than in the United States, whose economy was based to a large degree on cheap energy.

Suddenly the cost of heating, lighting, and cooling homes zoomed (between 1973 and 1975 utility bills rose an average of 48 percent and heating fuel costs rose 68.3 percent), and the nation was forced into energy consciousness. By 1976 solar energy, previously regarded as rather exotic, in some areas had become competitive with electricity for heating houses, and by 1978 there were over thirty thousand homes that got at least part of their energy from solar power, compared to under 300 in 1972.

The architectural changes necessary to provide solar energy changed the face of many new houses. Collector panels appeared on roofs, windows became greenhouselike, and walls were constructed of adobe, brick, or concrete—all good heat absorbers and insulators.

Those of us living in conventional homes suddenly became experts on insulation and those of us who had ready access to supplies of wood discovered the energy savings of woodburning stoves. Fireplaces that had been bricked up in modernization during the 1950s were unbricked, and curtains became appreciated as draft preventers as well as decorative elements.

The home-furnishings industry was no less affected. Factory running costs rose and so did the cost of raw materials—especially the until now cheap plastics and synthetics, for all had petrochemical bases. The price difference between them and the natural materials—wool, cotton, and wood—narrowed sharply.

But in spite of the constantly rising costs of home furnishings, Americans had never been more interested in their home surroundings. Partly it was because as inflation raised the cost of a night out, a weekend away, or a holiday abroad to prohibitive heights, we were all spending more time at home. And partly it was because, as the world outside seemed more and more insecure, we turned to our homes for reassurance.

All these elements encouraged many to hail Minimalism and High Tech as stylish low-budget answers but others developed fresh yearnings for "luxurious" furnishings as compensation for their changed lifestyle. Today, as we tackle the 1980s, there is a definite move back to the old-fashioned comforts of home—

soft upholstery, pastel but clear colors, and warm textures.

The rise in oil prices and the ensuing inflation also had less direct effects on how our homes looked. In a newly uncertain world where traditional investments no longer seemed blue-chip, there was an almost out-of-control rush to antiques and art as an alternative to stocks and bonds. Throughout the 1970s, in almost every category, more and more objects sold at higher and higher prices: eighteenth- and nineteenth-century furniture; Art Nouveau and Art Deco pieces; old-master, nineteenth-century, and modern paintings—almost anything that was old and a lot that wasn't.

This huge surge in art and antiques as investments is best reflected in the great success of the world's leading auction houses—such as Sotheby Parke Bernet, Christie's, and Phillips—during the 1970s.

Predating the energy crunch—but later given added impetus by it—were other enthusiasms that changed interior design. America discovered nature, health, and nutrition.

All three had their genesis in the hippie and flower-children movements of the late 1960s. True, their "dropping out" of society and penchant for communal living and drugs did not appeal to most Americans, but their desire to return to the basics of the land did strike a chord—especially when the energy crisis brought a new awareness that the earth's resources were finite—and initiated a consequent concern with ecology. Health food, organic foods, and "real" materials such as wool, cotton, and linen held increasing appeal.

This return to nature manifested itself in two ways. First, natural materials were used in their natural colors, producing a more neutral decorating palette. Second, everyone who had a small plot of earth, or even a balcony or window box, suddenly started gardening.

Hours were spent poring over seed catalogs and planning a vegetable garden that would feed a family of four for a year. Those who didn't have gardens brought nature indoors. Indoor plants had been of growing importance since houses were "opened up" in the 1950s, but now minigreenhouses were hung from kitchen windows, indoor plants became larger and were lit like sculpture, and exotic and flowering plants became an integral part of every decor. Everyone wanted greenery—ficus trees, palms, cymbidium orchids, ferns. Boston ferns were so ubiquitous that in 1978 one shelter magazine banned pictures of them from its pages.

The obsession with health turned bathrooms into exercise rooms and spas. "The smallest room in the house" started to expand, breaking through walls and taking over a guest room or part of the master bedroom to accommodate exercise benches and equipment, Jacuzzi whirlpool baths, even reading and relaxation areas. Fixtures became colorful and/or exotic, and after years of efficient showering, Americans discovered the bath, which, whether sunken or raised, made of porcelain, marble, or tile, now increased in size, and was very often placed by a window with a view, as its Sybaritic potential was recognized.

Nutrition made cooking chic. By the end of the 1970s, the kitchen without a food processor wasn't worth its salt and we turned away from convenience foods to build repertoires of *nouvelle cuisine* and Chinese or Italian specialties. Although an increasing belief that "you are what you eat" started this movement, inflation, as it made eating-out progressively more expensive, contributed its mite, and as a result kitchens changed drastically.

During the 1950s and 1960s kitchens had become smaller as they became more efficient but now, with host and hostess cooking, there was a move back to the large eat-in kitchen where guests could enjoy a drink, chat with their hosts as they worked, and generally enjoy the performance.

So far, all these causes and effects are continuing in the 1980s, although if anything is changing, it is that all the different design styles are merging slightly. Minimalists are coming to see the virtue of a few more objects and a little more color, while collectors and traditionalists are preferring visual clarity over clutter and are paring down their possessions.

But at the moment the 1980s, like the 1970s, are a time, as described by Paul Goldberger, the architecture critic of *The New York Times*, when "decorating might be described as 'Anything goes if you do it well enough.'"

McMillen itself continued to change in the 1960s and 1970s. The firm kept its reputation for the longevity of its staff, but a new tradition had begun—that of some of its decorators successfully moving out on their own. In 1963 Albert Hadley had left to join "Sister" Parish and her firm became Parish-Hadley, as it is today. By 1970 Kevin McNamara and Tom Buckley had started their own firms in New York and Los Angeles, respectively.

By now, also, there was increasing speculation that Eleanor Brown's retirement could not be far in the future. However, Mrs. Brown was still capably minding the store. In 1969 she had had discussions with David Hicks, the English designer, about his making his American base at McMillen. These came

In the late 1960s and early 1970s certain furnishings became chic, whether because they were modern classics or just cheap and cheerful. LEFT: One of the great modern classics, the leather-and-rosewood Eames chair and ottoman. ABOVE: Glass and chrome were cheerful and relatively cheap.

to nothing, but Mark Hampton, an American colleague of Mr. Hicks's, did join the firm.

Then in 1972, realizing that the contract department was not achieving its potential, Eleanor Brown hired Luis Rey, an architectural engineer. His account of his interview with her shows that age had not lessened her shrewd business sense.

"Mrs. Brown had heard of me through a friend and called me. I had been to the Parsons School of Design, so I knew about McMillen and its reputation and I didn't think I'd be interested because I had no interest in decoration. But I thought it would be only courteous to go and see her.

"She told me that she was concerned about the future of McMillen in the sense that there weren't many young designers there and because the company's strength was in traditional work. She felt a need for greater strength on the contemporary side.

"She also said that although McMillen had been doing more corporate work than ever before, it was still mainly for clients whose homes they had worked on and they had confined themselves to doing things like the president's office or a boardroom—in other words, isolated rooms within the corporate structure.

Other design icons were (*right*) Marcel Breuer's leather-and-tubular-steel "Wassily" chair and (*above*) Eero Saarinen's molded plastic pedestal table.

" 'We are a large firm in residential decoration,' she told me, 'but we are not a large firm when it comes to competing with architects for corporate work.' She wanted McMillen to be able to tackle the largest corporate jobs and she wanted me to reorganize the contract department so that it could.

"That intrigued me, but I still hesitated because I had no interest in residential design then. But they had already successfully completed a contract to do several floors of the Salomon Brothers' brokerage firm in New York, and other large contract jobs were in the offing. That changed my mind, but I remember that Mrs. Brown and I agreed it would be a gamble for both of us."

It was a gamble that paid off for both, for Luis Rey is now the vice-president in charge of a contract department that accounts for 50 percent of McMillen's business—and he is a convert to residential design, having found that it is creatively more satisfying than commercial work.

But although Eleanor Brown could still analyze acutely and act decisively, it was apparent that she was slowing down and that, even though she could still walk up and down four flights of stairs with ease and spot a loose carpet or a less than perfect seam at a glance, she could not continue to shoulder the administrative business of her company.

In the bedroom, shapes of things to come: the now ubiquitous pharmacy lamp (*above*) near the fireplace and Parsons table (*left*) by the bed.
OPPOSITE PAGE: Pots and pans were out in the open, hanging from a pegboard, while an Andy Warhol silkscreen print of Marilyn Monroe inspired the chef.

The staff and Mrs. Brown's family agreed that changes would have to be made. Deciding what the changes should be was another matter. It was a painful period for everyone concerned. Eventually, after much, often acrimonious, discussion among the family and the senior staff, it was decided in 1976 to restructure the company. Mrs. Brown was to become chairman, but who was to take her place as president? Betty Sherrill thinks that Mrs. Brown had looked for years for a man to take over. But neither John Drews nor Luis Rey wanted the job.

Finally, as this period of indecision became dangerously long, Betty Sherrill took the bull by the horns. "Apart from John and Luis, neither of the other senior staff members—Ethel Smith and Marion Morgan—wanted to take it on. I wasn't sure that I did either, but someone had to do something. So, I simply said, 'All right, if no one else wants it, I'll do it.' And that was that."

Mrs. Sherrill took over amid some skepticism. "The others," she laughs now, "like to say I flew by the seat of my pants. But I haven't made a mistake yet."

Far from it. It rapidly became apparent that Betty Sherrill possessed not only educated good taste and a flair for public relations (attributes that had always been apparent during her twenty-five years with McMillen) but also acute business acumen: the same combination of talents, in fact, that had made Eleanor

Brown successful. Once she became president, her administrative abilities quickly showed, and the enormous internal changes that have taken place at McMillen during the last six years have been mainly at her instigation.

"I think it must have been very hard for Mrs. Brown," Betty Sherrill admits. "Her father had told her never to take in any partners, and the company had always been run by her in a completely autocratic way. Now it's not run like that at all. We have regular meetings and we all discuss everything."

In 1978 Mrs. Sherrill did what had always been regarded as impossible: she persuaded Mrs. Brown to move McMillen's offices from her beloved townhouse to modern offices two blocks away. "I know it hurt Mrs. Brown very deeply to leave that house," Betty Sherrill recognizes. "She always said that we'd move out of it over her dead body. But the townhouse was far too small—we had offices across the street as well and wasted an awful lot of time going back and forth. And the neighborhood was changing. We had a massage parlor next door. I think that was the last straw, even for Mrs. Brown, who had always believed that one could rise above one's environment."

The new offices, all on one level, were designed by Luis Rey, and their horizontal openness reinforced the changes that had been wrought by the corporate restructuring.

The vertical organization of the townhouse, with everyone separated into small offices, had supported the way the firm operated for its first fifty years—each decorator working independently under the aegis of Eleanor Brown.

Now the designers work more as a group. Each has a say in the way the company is run and the new offices encourage joint efforts on design projects as well. Ideas and suggestions flow more freely, and both John Drews and Luis Rey, who even ten years ago would have been confined strictly to designing backgrounds, are now decorating as well.

There is still continuity, however. Eleanor Brown's original concept of having a design department to decide the layout, mood, and image of a room and decorators to then furnish and color it accordingly is still the backbone of any McMillen project.

The internal upheavals, however, were not allowed to affect the company's work. Under Luis Rey the contract department expanded as Mrs. Brown wished. The original Salomon Brothers' contract in New York grew to include their offices in Atlanta, Boston, Chicago, Los Angeles, Philadelphia, St. Louis, Cleveland, Dallas, and London—all done under the supervision of Marion Morgan.

Other major contracts have come from Mobil Oil, Morgan Stanley, Chemical Bank, St. Regis Paper Company, Paine Webber, Bache Halsey Stuart Shields, Hill Samuel, and for the executive floor of the John F. Kennedy Library in Dorchester, Massachusetts.

Eleanor Brown's foresight has certainly paid off, for the greatly increased volume of commercial work has helped shield McMillen from the effects of the recession during recent years. The past decade did not see any reduction in the number of private clients coming to McMillen but they did, by and large, have less money to spend.

In addition to that bald fact, the 1970s also saw a great increase in the number of prestigious designers at work. Most of McMillen's postwar competitors were still going strong; they had been joined by the several McMillen "alumni" now in business for themselves; and there was yet another new generation of talent entering the lists. Joe D'Urso, Bob Patino and Vincente Wolf, John Saladino, Bob Bray, and Michael Schaible were all making reputations in the Minimal or Modern idioms while David Easton and Michael La Rocca, Georgina Fairholme, and Carleton Varney, to name but a few, were concentrating on traditional interiors.

Nor was decorating solely the province of professionals anymore. Fabrics and furniture that had once been exclusively "to the trade" were being mass-marketed, and as the do-it-yourself movement developed, thousands of women—"ten-percenters," as the professionals disparagingly call them—were taking just enough courses to get a decorator's card and then making wholesale raids on design showrooms all over the country.

But McMillen's reputation stood them in good stead and, as usual, the company made sure it kept a high profile.

In 1970 it was one of four firms which each decorated an area of New York's Metropolitan Museum of Art for its centennial ball. Each area was to evoke a specific time: 1870, 1900, 1930, and 1970. McMillen was assigned 1900 and turned the museum's Blumenthal Patio into a *fin de siècle* extravaganza that was featured in *House & Garden*, one of twenty McMillen interiors that were featured in that magazine during the ensuing ten years.

In 1973 McMillen decorated a room in the first Kips Bay Showhouse—now an annual, and very successful, decorators' showcase organized each May in a New York house for the benefit of the Kips Bay Boy's Club.

The firm's "political" work, begun with Blair House and the White House during the Kennedy and Johnson administrations, continued during the presidency of Gerald Ford.

When Anne Armstrong was appointed ambassador to Great Britain, Betty Sherrill helped her reorganize Winfield House, the ambassador's official London residence, in a hurry. "Walter Annenberg, Mrs. Armstrong's predecessor, had hung the walls with his own art collection which he had, of course, taken with him. When we arrived, the walls were bare, with marks that showed where pictures had been; all the china cabinets were empty, and the rooms were less than half furnished—again because the Annenbergs had used a lot of their own things.

"And the Queen Mother was coming to tea. We spent the day frantically pulling things out of the basement and down from the bedrooms. An hour before the Queen Mother was due to arrive, I was downstairs in my curlers arranging flowers to fill the gaps that remained. The staff thought I was mad. It was one of our fastest jobs."

Then in 1974 McMillen was asked to decorate the State Dining room at the White House for the banquet in honor of the late President Anwar Sadat of Egypt. Betty Sherrill described it—and its repercussions: "President Sadat had never been to the White House before, but apparently he was a great admirer of the Wild West. President Ford had borrowed a private collector's Remingtons and Russells to hang on the walls and we used the bronzes as centerpieces for the tables. We had Indian-patterned tablecloths made, and used dried flower arrangements.

"It must have been successful because afterwards President Ford asked if we'd do more dinners. I told him that we didn't really do parties but that I'd do the state dinner when Queen Elizabeth came. I was half joking and thought no more about it until Anne Armstrong called me one day and said, 'You'd better get down here. The President wants to discuss the dinner for the queen.'

"When I got to Washington, President Ford told me he'd decided to have the dinner in the Rose Garden. 'That's fine,' I said, 'what size is the tent?' 'Tent?' questioned Mrs. Ford. 'We're not having a tent.' No tent, maybe no party, I thought. 'It might be planned for June but it can still rain and you can't suddenly move four hundred people inside.'

"So they agreed to a tent but offered me an old pink-and-white-striped one. 'No way,' I protested. 'This is the White House and I want a brand-new white tent.' We got it, too.

"We recolored a beautiful Scalamandre English flowered chintz for the tablecloths, with centerpieces of English roses and wildflowers like Queen Anne's lace. We had to raid half the gardens in Washington to get those. Somebody wanted to hang three crystal chandeliers in the tent—can you imagine that? But we got big Noguchi paper lanterns instead that gave a soft pink light.

"I asked Jimmy Goslee, a very talented flower arranger, to come down and help me. We had to do the whole thing in two days and the flowers, of course, on the day of the dinner. We also had to do all the flowers for Blair House and the White House, and it was frantic. We were decorating one room ahead of the Queen as she moved through the White House.

"And thank goodness for the tent, because twenty minutes before the queen came out, there was a downpour. We had the Marines manning a bucket brigade until just before she arrived. It stopped, just like that, when she came out."

But, inevitably, McMillen garnered its greatest publicity when it celebrated its fiftieth anniversary in November 1974. Eleanor Brown used the occasion to counter the celebrations of her success by voicing a few mild complaints in *The New York Times*. Yes, she agreed, McMillen was working all over the United States, in Europe, and even the Middle East, but they were projects she never expected to see. At the age of eighty-four, she lamented, "I do very little traveling."

Yes, the diversity and sheer amount of McMillen's work, past and present, was cause for congratulation. But it had also become a cause of frustration. "I feel my creativity has given way to administration." In another interview, she also reiterated her—and McMillen's—design philosophy, principles that had stayed constant throughout the half-century. "In decorating," she acknowledged, "functionalism at all costs is the goal of many self-styled modernists, yet there is another school to which McMillen subscribes that holds that beauty and charm must play a part as well. For man must have something about him that identifies his house with his own personality and, thankfully, not many personalities can be called strictly functional."

Their increasing expertise in the modern vernacular brought McMillen a new generation of clients during these years. Some were children, or even grandchildren, of clients, but others were newly wealthy businessmen or entrepreneurs who came to McMillen for the social cachet and credibility the firm could bestow as well as for the high quality of its work.

For one phenomenon of the 1970s was the countrywide rise of designer chic. The growing—and continuing—penchant for wearing designer clothes emblazoned with designer initials so that their status could not be missed quite naturally spread to interior design. Who had "done" one's house became as important to some as what was in it.

But though the name of the company may have taken on a new fashionability, its work has not. Indeed, its new clients do not want trend-setting interiors. They want the McMillen hallmarks in a well-bred, up-to-date environment that will last, whatever style of design they choose.

Clients come to McMillen today because they know that, whatever the design idiom, McMillen has an expert in it. And it is this, as much as anything, that keeps McMillen preeminent in its field almost sixty years after it was founded.

So as Eleanor Brown, now in her nineties, takes an increasingly less active part in her company, she has no qualms about its continuing success. McMillen may owe much of that success to her creative and financial acumen, and it will certainly always reflect her attitudes, but just as she had always planned, it has a life of its own.

The 1970s saw the "discovery" of the bathroom as a room. Like most things, it had happened before. This luxurious bathroom was designed in the 1930s. The crystal dressing table was made for Marie Antoinette.

BELOW: A travertine-floored terrace leads from the house to the swimming pool and on to the Gulf. The furniture under the awning is rattan with cotton-covered seats and cushions; the furniture close to the pool is made of metal and plastic.

Louis McMillen, Eleanor McMillen Brown's son, was the architect of this house, which was recently built on the Persian Gulf. When the owners asked him if he could recommend any interior designers, he mentioned that his mother was thought to be pretty good. On the strength of this modest mention, McMillen was hired and invited to design a basically Western interior incorporating Middle Eastern decorative elements—the same combination that had been successfully used in the architecture of the house (*above left*).

TOP LEFT: Since the sun streams through a wall of windows in the living room, colors were kept in the cool citrus spectrum.

ABOVE RIGHT: In a shaded study, a bold Jack Lenor Larsen print on chairs and sofas picks up the colors of the Persian rug.

On these pages, a portfolio that illustrates the eclecticism of the 1970s.
RIGHT: Fabric shirred on walls and into a sunburst effect on the ceiling makes this room look like a romantic, exotic tent.

ABOVE: A traditionally furnished dining room given the contemporary chic of wall-to-wall chocolate-brown-and-white trim.

TOP LEFT: For a young couple, a simple contemporary treatment using modular furniture. Teal-blue tones in the painting are picked up in the cushion covers.

FAR RIGHT: Black and white make a strong impression in this small entrance hall.

ABOVE: Bathrooms gained importance and became larger. McMillen designed this oversize marble tub as the focus of a bath/dressing/exercise room.

Two ways with tradition:

TOP LEFT: A softly furnished living room with pale striéed walls and pastel patterns.

BOTTOM LEFT: The same idea, but with a much stronger palette.

TOP RIGHT: An assortment of furniture in a country bedroom is unified by use of the same color over all.

CENTER RIGHT: The severity of the modern Italian glass-and-brass table and chairs is softened by the antique Ushak rug on which they stand.

ABOVE: A small study uses wood and neutral colors in International Modernist style.

This classic yet contemporary design that comes close to Minimalism is an essay on the diagonal. Color is kept neutral but deep in tone. Suede-covered sofas are built into platforms that have carpet running up and over them. Other furniture is either modern and classic—the side and arm chairs are Mies van der Rohe designs—or custom-built, with strong geometry and lacquered surfaces. Modern art is the decorative element here.

TOP: The living room looks out onto a small sculpture garden. Inside is a Dubuffet. Mirrored tiles add height to the ceiling.
ABOVE LEFT: Marble runs diagonally across the entrance hall and up the stairway. The painting is by Picasso.
ABOVE CENTER: In the dining area, the table opens out envelope-style to seat ten. The paintings are by Adolph Gottlieb and Jean Dubuffet.

ABOVE RIGHT: Sliding red doors can be pulled across to make one end of the study a guest room. Cabinets between the doors conceal stereo equipment and a television. Over them hangs a small Rauschenberg.

Photographs by Norman McGrath

Every year top decorators contribute their talents for the benefit of the Kips Bay Boys Club, a New York charity. Each time the organizers manage to find a house that not only is large enough for the event but also happens to be empty for one reason or another. Each decorator designs one room, and the resulting exhibit is opened to the public for a small fee

in the spring. The Kips Bay House, as the exhibition is known, has gained the deserved reputation of being the place to pick up the newest ideas in decorating. The rooms McMillen contributed to several of the houses are shown here.

TOP: McMillen's 1975 room came with magnificent paneling and was furnished, following its warm tones, as a living/dining room with leather and wood seating in the living area, teak Chinese-style dining chairs, and a pewter-lacquered dining table. The pastels of the dhurrie rug lightened the effect of an abundance of dark woods.

ABOVE LEFT: The 1977 room was small and had no architectural distinction. McMillen opened it up by keeping the center clear and using light furniture. The room's dull banana-leaf-pattern wallpaper was hidden behind a sharp raspberry-color Ultrasuede.

ABOVE RIGHT: In 1979 McMillen produced a High Tech design with glamour. Sharp-edged black furniture stood out in high relief against a background of muted beiges, grays, and pinks. The chaise is the Le Corbusier classic with its pad removed; the three metal-and-wood sculptures are by Susan Rodgers.

Photographs by Norman McGrath and Jaime Ardiles-Arce

Luis Rey, a vice-president of McMillen, designed his own apartment to make the most of space and budget—both were limited.

RIGHT: In the living room, furniture consists of industrial-carpet-covered plywood cubes and rectangles. The cushions are covered in canvas duck, and the chair backs are sheets of plywood "slipcovered" in canvas. The painting is by Frank Faulkner.

As shown in the other three pictures, the bedroom/study cleverly does extra duty as a dining room. The bed (*above right*) lies on two carpet-covered plywood platforms, and another shallow platform runs around two sides of the room. On another wall (*left*) there is shelving with two pedestal tables used as a desk. ABOVE LEFT: For dinner parties, Mr. Rey stows the mattress in a closet, puts its platforms on the surround, moves the tables into place, and brings in extra "Cesca" chairs from the hall.

Photographs by Michael Dunne

Another design on a budget, this time in a loft belonging to the artist Frank Faulkner. Mr. Faulkner already owned some country antiques but wanted his large space made comfortable without clutter being added. The walls, beams, and exposed pipes were all painted white, a partition was built to make a contained kitchen (*right*), and the concrete floor was painted slate gray.

TOP: A banquette was built along one wall and gray carpeting was added to subtly define the seating area. The two round tables were made from car-wheel rims; they now support concrete cesspool covers. Faulkner's jewel-like paintings are on the walls.

Photographs by Michael Dunne

ABOVE LEFT: The seating area looks down the length of the loft past the dining area to a sliding wall that has a studio behind it. The expanse is broken by two kilim rugs.

ABOVE CENTER: A large French cheesemaking table stands against the kitchen partition. An elliptical lamp was made by placing an industrial safety lamp between two sheets of bristol board, which were then taped together at each end.

ABOVE RIGHT: Simplicity continues in the bedroom, where again no attempt was made to hide pipes. Visual interest comes from the placement of the bed on the diagonal, the geometry of the Faulkner painting, and the neon sculpture.

295

The pictures on this page show interiors from three homes that were all done by McMillen for the same clients.

RIGHT: The newest includes an indoor swimming pool. McMillen lessened the monolithic aspect of its concrete walls by extending the

sliding glass doors and designing Venetian moldings to go over them. Painting the walls pale peach dispelled any lingering clinical quality, and the whole effect is softly inviting.

TOP LEFT: The glamour of the 1930s was also evoked in the dining room of another house with white suede wall panels seamed in chrome, a white-lacquered dining table, and white leather chairs.

LEFT CENTER: In the client's apartment, McMillen dramatized the entrance hall with bronze mirrors and a bronze glass screen that creates a

break between the hall and the living area.

ABOVE LEFT AND RIGHT: In the living/dining room, banquettes provide maximum seating. To give the impression of maximum space, color is

monochromatic except for two bursts of red—in the dining table and the Robert Natkin painting.

Photographs by Michael Dunne

LEFT: The music room, part of the new addition, had no architectural detailing. All the moldings were designed by John Drews at McMillen. The furniture is mostly Louis XV and XVI, but the mantel is English. The apricot of the walls and curtains is picked up from that in the antique Sultanabad rug.

BELOW: The original entrance hall, with its checkerboard marble floor and gracefully curving staircase, only needed to be repainted.

The Houston house on this and the next two pages was furnished in the last two years. The present owners started by building an extension almost half as large again as the already existing structure. They then asked McMillen to decorate the whole house with fine antique furniture—an enormous challenge today, when truly fine antiques fetch stratospheric prices whenever they come onto the market. Although the budget was large, it was not limitless. However, Ethel Smith, who was in charge of the project, delved into her fifty years of experience and triumphed.

RIGHT: The dining room is lit by a rare original Adam chandelier. The candlesticks and candelabra are all the same Adam design though each was found in a different place. The dining table and sideboard are eighteenth-century English.

Photographs by Michael Dunne

RIGHT: The focus of the living room is a fine twelve-panel Coromandel screen.
BELOW: In the new atrium, McMillen adapted the design of the marble floor from that of England's Castle Howard. The floor also complements the pattern in the original entrance hall.

ABOVE: The kitchen, with its impressive *batterie de cuisine*, is large enough for the frequent large parties the owners give yet intimate enough for family cook-ins.
RIGHT: The owners wanted the basement made into a wine cellar where meals could also be served. They already had the huge round table; McMillen made the room a casual one with Windsor chairs, an old English pine cabinet, and walls hung with a French print fabric.

Photographs by Michael Dunne

LEFT: The Portuguese needlepoint rug was specially made for the master bedroom, and its soft pastel colors are picked up in the fabric used for the four-poster bed and curtains.

BELOW: In the master bathroom, the tub is enclosed in marble and surrounded by mirrored walls.

LEFT: The dressing rooms and clothes closets off the master bedroom were designed to make a large collection of clothes and accessories as easily visible and close to hand as they would be in a small boutique.

ABOVE: A guest bedroom is given a country French flavor by an *eau de Nil* and peach chinoiserie print used for the walls, curtains, and upholstered furniture.

Photographs by Michael Dunne

A young bachelor's haphazard collection of country furniture and accoutrements—old wicker, rugs, chests, baskets, walking sticks, and hats—are pulled together in this tiny New York brownstone and given some formality by the Etruscan design painted above the picture rail. But the net effect is still deliberately rural: this flat is used as a weekend retreat.

Photographs by Peter Vitali

In contrast, a couple moving from
country to city wanted a sophisticated reflection of their new environment.

Photograph by Michael Dunne

For a busy woman executive who didn't want to make structural changes in a boxlike modern apartment, McMillen designed a scheme of soft-toned efficiency and versatility. The room takes its delicate shades from the dhurrie rug. Lacquered cubes pull together or separate according to need, and the rattan armchairs can pull up alongside their juniors at the dining table.

Photographs by Michael Dunne

Finding their growing modern art collection at increasing odds with the antique furniture they had always lived with, its owners decided on drastic action: they moved into a modern house and sold most of their furniture. For their new environment, McMillen devised an unaggressively contemporary scheme (*above*) that incorporated the few antiques they kept as works of art—the dining table and chairs (*top left*), a walnut desk (*top center*), and an Early American settee and chair (*top right*).

Photographs by Michael Dunne

When McMillen moved from its townhouse into an office building, they took the opportunity, not surprisingly, to display the versatility of their work.

RIGHT: In the reception room, eighteenth-century French chairs sit at ease around a contemporary sofa, a Chinese table, and a black lacquer desk inlaid with mother of pearl.

LEFT: The conference-room table has a round marble top on a stainless-steel cylinder base. The chairs are made of leather and tubular steel.

TOP LEFT: The workrooms are businesslike and designed for efficiency, with a built-in place for everything. On the far wall, a reminder of times past: a blow-up of Van Day Truex's sketch of the old townhouse.

ABOVE: The entrance hall sets the tone: up-to-date, understated, elegant—the three attributes McMillen has carried with it for over sixty years.

Photographs by Richard Champion

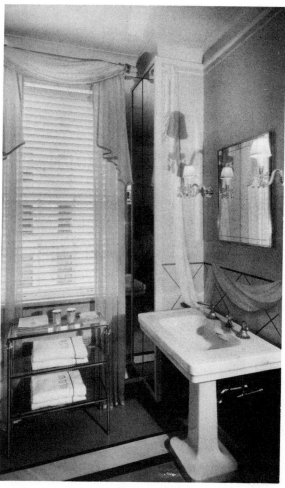

HERE AND ON THE NEXT TWO PAGES:
McMillen made great play with
trompe l'oeil in their thirties bathrooms. This one featured painted
muslin swags and stone jardinieres.
The curtains at the window (*above*)
were real; the ones over the mirror
(*right*) fake.

Photographs by Carl Klein Studios

Here, the *trompe l'oeil* is *faux marbre*, with lavish real satin hangings at the bath and windows.

If in all its diversity there is something that can be called the McMillen style, it is characterized by the fact that quality is evident in every fabric, every gimp, every paint job, and every accessory in every interior ever done by McMillen Inc. But nowhere is it more evident than in the interior architecture of a McMillen room. If a room doesn't already have good architecture when McMillen starts, it will have it by the time it's finished. Most of the architectural detailing in rooms the firm has worked on was created at the McMillen drawing board.

Their ability to design anything is extraordinary. If a client wants a French room that is what he will get and it will be accurate to whatever period he wants. Throughout the firm's existence, most of the staff have been graduates of the Parsons School of Design and, therefore, knowledgeable about period furnishings. But everyone who worked there before 1961 (when fading eyesight forced her retirement) had the added advantage of learning from Grace Fakes, who was expert in every antique period and, until her retirement in 1981, from Marion Morgan, a leading scholar of French eighteenth-century interior architecture and decoration. As a result, McMillen decorators all know exactly how high a chair rail or a sconce should be or what kind of molding is appropriate.

A great deal of McMillen's success can also be traced to Mrs. Brown's eye for talent and her desire always to surround herself with the best. She also realized that she would be limiting the business's potential if she concentrated on any particular style and, especially in the last twenty years when so many decorating options have flourished, has made a point of hiring decorators and designers of diverse tastes. It is this diversity that has allowed McMillen to tackle any style of work; whatever a client wanted, there has always been a specialist at McMillen.

And, thanks to the way Mrs. Brown organized the company, these diverse points of view have never become unruly. Kevin McNamara, a decorator who

McMillen is still decorating model rooms. This one was done for the Houston ballet ball in 1981.

Photograph by Jim Johnson

spent several years at McMillen in the 1960s, says, "Everyone there was an individual with a style all their own. But one of the phenomenons of Mrs. Brown was that even though we were all individualists, we all worked together."

The way it worked in the early days is basically the way it still works. A client would arrive having been, let's say, recommended to McMillen by a friend. Mrs. Brown (now it's Betty Sherrill) would discuss the client's needs and desires with her and then bring in the decorator and/or the designer whose taste most closely matched the client's. A scheme would be worked out, and once the client agreed to it, the team would go into action—decorator, designer, assistant, and secretary—with strong backup from the highly efficient bookkeeping and shipping departments. All was under the careful, but generally benevolent, eye of Eleanor Brown.

First, the design department would work out the layout, mood, and image of the room. Then the decorator in charge would furnish it accordingly. The design department's decisions were precise. If they had decreed light-colored walls, a marble floor, dark paneling, or eighteenth-century French style, the decorator could not come up with a scheme of dark-colored walls, wall-to-wall carpeting, white painted paneling, or eighteenth-century English style. But these boundaries still left the decorator great latitude in choosing specific colors, textures, fabrics, patterns, furniture, and accessories.

Kevin McNamara spent his seven years at McMillen as an assistant to both Ethel Smith and Betty Sherrill. He gives a pithy description of the life:

"There was a feeling that the business office really ran you as an assistant. Their purchase-order system is fantastic and their bookkeeping impeccable. You really had to please that bookkeeping department or they got after you.

"You got the estimates written and you got them approved in the bookkeeping department. They signed them and then the secretary typed them for you and you got them out to the clients. Then you started ordering and then you checked the orders. You would go round to the workrooms and you had to go every day and you had to check every seam on every sofa and if you didn't, it would catch up with you.

"Also, every day you had to go to the job and check construction, the painting, and so forth. You also shopped for schemes for the decorators.

"The first day I was there, I was sent out shopping and at four o'clock all the decorators assembled to see what I had found. I'd been all of one day in New York and I had to put on a presentation for them! They were very relaxed about it and told me

what they did and didn't like. But they really kept you hopping."

But McMillen offered a young decorator the very best of working conditions. John Drews, now a vice-president of the firm, remembers: "When I went there straight from Parsons in 1960, I didn't realize the luxury I would be working in. I had the opportunity to design *boiseries*, marble floors, furniture, things that many designers will never get the chance to do."

Kevin McNamara agrees. "I had very few of my own jobs, but the first day I was there, Tom Buckley, who was Grace Fakes's deputy, said, 'If you have any sense at all, you will shut up for two years and listen and learn.' It was a great piece of advice for me. I had no idea how good decorating could be until I went there. I saw quality I had no idea existed. Even being an assistant, you were getting the experience and seeing things you had never seen before. I'm sorry for people who haven't had that experience."

And there were certain rituals and certain dicta at McMillen, all of which reflected Mrs. Brown's personality.

Eleanor Brown believed that if you couldn't get your work done between nine and five, there was something wrong. Besides, she believed, everyone was entitled to a private life. Albert Hadley remembers, "You were never late for work. At exactly five o'clock, the office doors closed and at two minutes past, the alarm went on. Grace Fakes was the only person who ever went back to McMillen on a weekend. She would slip in sometimes, but Eleanor didn't like it much. She always felt she paid decent salaries and there was no need for anyone to work overtime."

Kevin McNamara adds, "There was a certain protocol there that was marvelous. You could not have a cup of coffee. It was not permitted. Tea was served at four o'clock in the afternoon and that was different. There were no paper cups on any desk.

"Mrs. Brown used to wear those bracelets that tinkle when you walk and you could hear them as she was coming to your desk. She would come in and sit down and have a cup of tea with you and go over your work. I always felt she let those bracelets tinkle so you'd be prepared for her when she arrived."

With this kind of close attention to everything that was going on in the company, it's not surprising that Eleanor Brown's design beliefs have always been evident in McMillen's work. Albert Hadley says, "Her own personal taste has always been for the late eighteenth century and for classical, formal, symmetrical interiors. There's an enormous sense of order about what she does but it's relaxed; things aren't always placed in pairs.

"She has a very intellectual sense, not just about

color and texture, but about the ability and function of things. There's no nonsense. Her fanciful side shows in other ways, through modern pictures, modern sculpture. The contemporary aspect of her work comes not so much through furniture but through the things that one brings to a well-organized space."

Eleanor Brown never became a fan of Bauhaus furniture, though she would work with it if it was required. Nor was she interested in the other end of the design spectrum—"fussy" furniture such as gilt Régence and Louis XIV—although, again, she'd use it if a client insisted. Her loves are Louis XVI, Directoire, and eighteenth-century Italian furniture, classically styled pieces in black and mahogany, and Egyptian Revival furniture. Favorite colors are yellow and black, but not autumnal schemes; she thinks they are dreary. She likes school of Paris paintings, late impressionists, and flower paintings of all sorts.

Mark Hampton, who was with McMillen in the 1970s, offers further pointers to the McMillen style. "Mrs. Brown likes simplified curtains. She has a very strict point of view about how windows should be done. You don't get into any monkey business around a window. She doesn't like fringe and you never hang a mirror over a sofa. Occasionally you'll find a room with a mirror built in over a banquette, but mirrors go over tables and chairs. And that's historically accurate. Mirrors never were hung over sofas."

Ben Flowers, another McMillen alumnus who now has his own firm in Washington, D.C., adds, "Curtains were always finished with a trim or a binding. They always had several interlinings, even if we were using an inexpensive fabric, so that they would hang right. We always took out ceiling light fixtures in bedrooms—that light is harsh and the fixtures usually unattractive. We frequently mirrored one wall of a hall to make a small space look bigger. When I was there in the early 1970s, the metal radiator covers in older apartments usually had about twenty coats of paint on them. We always stripped them and showed they were metal by brassing or chroming them. Usually brass. We used specially made medicine cabinets with a certain beveled edge and lights that would pop out.

"We always used the Carr sofa made by Thomas de Angelis. It was so soft that if you put a hand on an arm it sank down four inches. And we never used stripes on sofas. We used the Odom chair which has a tight back with a slight curve to it and curved arms that we wrapped and a very soft down seat."

McMillen is so successful, Ben Flowers believes, "because Mrs. Brown first of all had the know-how and the good taste. Then she got the right people. She always had a good business manager and she made the right contacts. She wasn't impressed by society but she had a few good friends and, right from the start, she gave them excellent service. They respected her opinions and her work.

"If ever there was a problem, it was corrected. If something like the color of a wall wasn't exactly right, McMillen repainted it at no cost to the client. Sometimes McMillen would do that before the client objected. Everyone was very aware of what was right and what was wrong and everyone wanted it right."

Or, as Mrs. Brown once said to Kevin McNamara, "I'm a rich lady, Kevin, and it's a very good thing, because I've always been able to run this firm the way I wanted to."

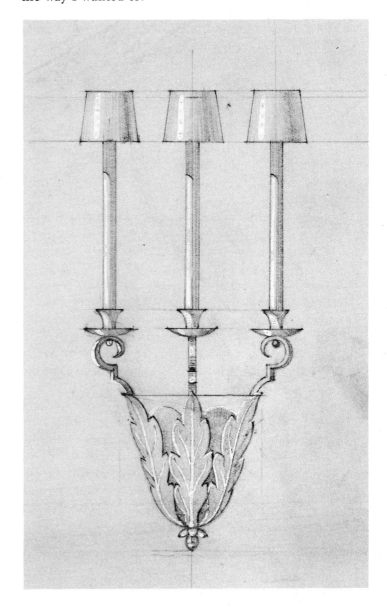

Betty Sherrill is a native of New Orleans, something of a daredevil, and the daughter of an architect. Blond and petite, she has retained her Southern accent and charm but also has the full measure of ambition and high achievement that might be expected of a woman who both flew planes and raced sailboats in her teens. Her father encouraged her in these exploits and she followed in his professional footsteps to a certain extent by deciding to study interior design.

She came to New York to the Parsons School of Design but quit halfway through, in 1951, when she married a young stockbroker.

"I opened my own company, Elizabeth Sherrill Interiors, but had to close it after a year. I was working for friends and ended up doing everything for free. And I always forgot to collect the resale tax and things like that."

So in 1952 she just came and knocked at McMillen's door and asked for a job. "I was pregnant, but I was homesick for New Orleans and I really wanted a job. Mrs. Brown tried very hard not to hire me because I was pregnant and she thought I was too social, would be out every night and never in the office.

"I just kept on coming back and, eventually, when the 'Paris 1952' exhibition opened, she needed some extra help and I got my foot in the door. I worked as an assistant for every decorator in the firm and got fired by each of them but I survived."

She survived so well, in fact, that today she is McMillen's president. She admits she is still the kind of decorator who prefers to start scheming around furnishings and colors rather than to begin from an abstract concept. But she credits McMillen with broadening her design outlook as well as giving her the opportunity to discover her considerable business acumen.

Her colleagues also credit her with being the best client-getter—and client-keeper—in the business, and she is a walking encyclopedia of their lives. Marriages, divorces, remarriages, children, and grandchildren are all filed neatly in their current order in her mind. But never to be discussed as gossip. For her, this is merely necessary information. For these clients have frequently become friends, and during the last thirty years it is to her that they have turned to reorganize their homes when their lives have changed.

In 1979 Ethel Smith celebrated her golden anniversary with McMillen. "I arrived in 1929, right at the start of the Depression. Terrific timing!"

After her education at boarding school in New York, she was led to interior design as a profession by an aunt who had always wanted to be a decorator. "But in those days, she wasn't allowed to work. When I went to the Parsons School, it was she who chaperoned me during the year we spent in Europe."

Today Ethel Smith still handles a full roster of clients, both residential and commercial. She has a head full of rooms and, right from the beginning, can visualize how a finished room will look, down to the last ashtray. She has never been surprised by the result.

"I learned that very early on, before I came to McMillen. I worked for a woman called Margaret Owen, who had a tiny one-room office. There was no room to bring in five or six samples of everything to see which went best with what. You had to learn to do it in your head as you went round the showrooms."

Ethel Smith is so good at this that she can create successful schemes for rooms she has never seen and clients she has never met. "Sometimes you get to see the rooms after they are finished and, sure enough, they look exactly as you knew they would."

Her forte is the traditional, comfortable house with quality antiques and soft colorings. She is credited with finding the "McMillen table"—a still contemporary small end table of glass on a chrome spiral. "I saw the original in 1950 in the window of a small shop in New York. I remember thinking it would be very useful so I bought one and we've copied it in various finishes ever since." In fact, very few McMillen interiors have been done since then without at least one.

John Drews

John Drews grew up with a flair for art, but it was during his spell in the air force that he started working as an interior designer. "I worked nights at a base near Albany, Georgia, so I had my days free. After a summer lying around the swimming pool I couldn't stand the boredom any longer, so I went to the one decorating firm in Albany and offered my services, really just for the experience. I worked there for the rest of the two years I was in the service and when that was over, the owners told me that if I wanted to pursue interior design as a profession I should go to Parsons.

"When I graduated I sent my résumé to about ten decorators and didn't hear from one of them. Eventually I started to call them and McMillen asked me to come and see them. Mrs. Brown kept my portfolio and they called three days later to say they'd hire me and how much did I want. I'd heard that they didn't pay much so I asked for $45. This was in 1959. They offered me $75 a week, so I jumped at it."

John Drews was hired to work in the design department under Grace Fakes. "In those days, the design department was strictly that. I remember Mrs. Brown telling me when I was hired that, although I'd be in decorating, I wouldn't be a decorator. And that was true. We did the designs for moldings, floors, window treatments, and so on, and then the decorators took them and finished the jobs."

Today, as a vice-president, John Drews is the head designer at McMillen but he also decorates. He doesn't have time to take more than one or two clients as his own, for he is still responsible for creating the backgrounds for all the work that goes through the firm. And with the quality and quantity of his work, that's time-consuming. Much of it is still traditional, and everything, even a dressing table, is thoroughly researched. Also, as more and more corporate work comes McMillen's way, the work load has increased.

"Most architects today don't have backgrounds in traditional design but that's what a lot of corporations want. We do know the details of period design and that's one reason our corporate work has increased. Eight or nine years ago, we might have had two commercial jobs going at any one time, but now it's more than ten."

All these, whether decorated by Betty Sherrill, Ethel Smith, or Mary Louise Guertler, are defined and fleshed out at John Drews's drawing board.

Luis Rey

Luis Rey works separately but in tandem with John Drews. He is credited with giving the firm much of the expertise in modern design vernaculars that it has acquired during the last ten years.

Before he joined McMillen in 1972, his work lay solely in the commercial field of offices and institutions. His interest lies in the structure of space, not in its decoration, and his spare, precise, but soft interiors are now very much a part of McMillen's design vocabulary. He is also a graduate of the Parsons School, having gone to study there from his native Peru in 1962.

Luis Rey was not sure at the beginning that he had made the right decision in coming to McMillen. "It took time for me to adjust. I had thought I would not be involved in the traditional work the company did. But I had to be and that was a shock. But today I'm very pleased it happened. It made me much less narrow-minded.

"I also had to get used to doing residential work, which I had never tried before. Now I prefer it to commercial jobs. It's more creative in both the materials and styles you can use. In commercial work, you are invariably dealing with a committee, which means more compromising than you get with an individual client. Committees are less adventurous."

It was partly the lack of creative adventurousness that led him to decide he didn't want to be president of McMillen. "I would have had to concentrate on other areas—business, public relations, and promotion—that I'm not very good at. My strengths are in creative design and the work of actually installing a house or office."

Mary Louise Guertler arrived at McMillen in 1965 via the now familiar training of the Parsons School and after three years in the interior design department of Bloomingdale's. "I came as Mrs. Sherrill's assistant and I've never thought of leaving.

"I like the backup. I think you limit yourself unless you have a large organization. You can't take on the big exciting jobs that we do. And you have so much interaction of ideas here. You can ask questions or you can contribute if someone else has a question."

Mrs. Guertler's work spans both the traditional and the modern, residential and commercial. But whichever the style of the moment, she says, "I really like a clean, direct look. Contemporary but with classical balance and symmetry, and I like warm colors like salmon and coral. In fact, I've been kidded that I can't do a room without putting coral in it somewhere."

Working alongside the senior designers are three others who, it is expected, will one day join their ranks. For, as always, McMillen is looking to its future and has chosen young designers of diversity.

In keeping with the McMillen tradition, Fred Cannon is a graduate of the Parsons School. His design strength is also in the McMillen tradition—it's traditional—and as Ethel Smith's right arm he has been closely involved with most of the "grand" interiors done by the firm during the last ten years.

Betsy Shaw studied art history, and then worked for magazines before becoming a decorator for a now defunct company. In 1975 she set up her own business and, in 1977, came to McMillen because, she says, "I can do more here than I could on my own." Her work is in the mainsteam of interior design today, neither strictly traditional nor completely contemporary.

Terry Gelfand grew up playing among the furniture—antiques and modern classics—in her mother's decorating shop in South Africa. She studied art and architecture in Italy and France, and joined McMillen two months after she arrived in New York in 1978. While she says her style is classic in terms of quality, her approach is contemporary. "I'm not keen on floral chintzes: I like fabric to be muted. I do like color but I prefer it plain."

Index

Index

Page numbers set in italics indicate pages with captions.